Google™ Search Complete!

Tips, Tricks and Shortcuts for Better Searches and Better Results

Kirk Paul Lafler
Charles Edwin Shipp

Odyssey

Press

Lafler
Google
BETTER
INDEXING
Shipp
algorithm
tricks
Complete
Page
HUMMINGBIRD
SHORTCUTS
BRIN
ALGORITHM
ORGANIZING
SHIPP
RESULTS
shortcuts
crawling
tips
better
search
Brin

Tips, Tricks and Shortcuts for Better Searches and Better Results

Published by Odyssey Press
A Division of Software Intelligence Corporation

ISBN-13: 978-0692285169
ISBN-10: 0692285164

Odyssey Press, a division of Software Intelligence Corporation,
Spring Valley, California USA.

Author Bios

Kirk Paul Lafler is consultant, founder and CEO of Software Intelligence Corporation (1983-present), an IT, database, consulting and training solutions provider to users around the world. Kirk has worked with a variety of database, programming languages and analytical software technologies since 1979. He has served in consulting, project management, application development, data science, and training roles to organizations worldwide providing analytics, database administration, performance tuning, programming and technical support using leading programming languages, analytical and database technologies on mainframe and server-based mini and microcomputers including SAS, R, SYSTEM 2000, Oracle, Sql-Server, DB2, MySQL, COBOL, JCL, FORTRAN, ISPF Dialog, MemSQL, NuoDB and others. Kirk has written several books including PROC SQL: Beyond the Basics Using SAS, Second Edition (SAS Institute. 2013), Power SAS: A Survival Guide (Apress. 2002), Power AOL: A Survival Guide (Apress. 2002) and more than five hundred professional papers and articles for conference proceedings, journals and other scholarly publications. Kirk is an Invited speaker, keynote presenter, mentor, conference leader and trainer to user groups, conferences, events and meetings; recipient of nearly two dozen "Best" contributed paper, hands-on workshop (HOW), and poster awards; adviser and instructor for the Specialized Certificate in SAS Programming curriculum at the University of California San Diego Extension; and has served on numerous Advisory Boards.

Charles Edwin Shipp is consultant, founder and CEO of Consider Consulting Corporation (2010-present), a global provider of analytical applications, consulting services and technical support solutions. Charlie's technical and business experience involves working on mainframe, mini and microcomputers designing, developing and testing program code using a variety of software languages including SAS software, JMP software, FORTRAN, JCL, and other languages since 1970. He is the co-author of three books including, Quick Results with SAS/GRAPH Software and more than two hundred professional papers and articles for conference proceedings, journals and other scholarly publications; is an invited speaker, conference leader and trainer at hundreds of user group conferences, events and meetings; and is the recipient of a dozen "Best" contributed paper and poster awards. Charlie is currently involved as an eBook author, curriculum designer and developer, instructor, smart device app developer, sasCommunity.org Advisory Board member, and mentor, among his many other interests.

Google, Google Search and other Google products and services are the registered trademarks of Google Inc., Mountain View, California, USA.

Dedications

To Darlynn and Ryan,
for your love and support!
I love you both!

In loving memory of my mother and father
for their love and support,
and for encouraging me to pursue my dreams,
and believe anything is possible!

KPL

~ ~ ~

To Lynnette, the love of my life,
our wonderful son, daughters,
and grandchildren. Be great.

To professional and home researchers
who will benefit from this Book and eBook.

CES

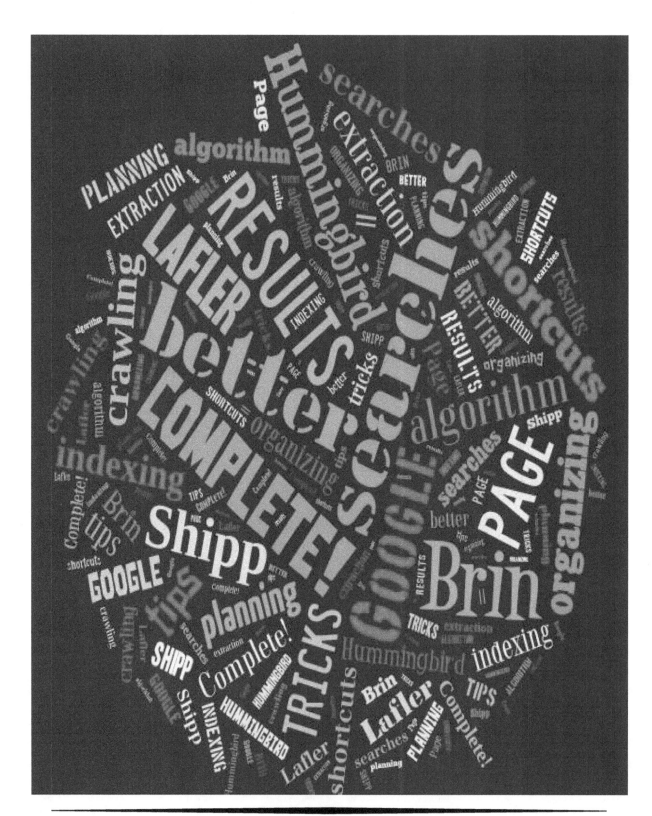

Section and Chapter Contents

Example Contents

Example Contents (continued)

Example Contents (continued)

Example Contents (continued)

Chapter 10 Continued

Section I

Better Searches = Better Results

~ Chapter 1 ~

Speed, Accuracy, Organization and Reliability

The World of Search and Google

Google® search (www.google.com) is the world's most popular and widely-used search engine. As the premier search tool on the Internet today, anyone can use its power to find practically anything, and in almost any form, they are looking for. We'll provide insights into how Google search works and illustrate numerous search tips, techniques and shortcuts that can be used to find websites, people, businesses, articles of interest, reference works, information tools, directories, PDFs, images, current news stories, user and professional groups, and other content to produce search results quickly and easily.

Speed, Accuracy, Organization and Reliability

It's a fact that millions of users from all walks of life turn to Google more than any other search engine for their search needs. As the world's information continues to grow to astronomical levels, Google, and its proprietary software, organizes and indexes this information by making it useful and accessible to anyone using a browser. Google's incredibly fast and thorough search engine provides users with the speed, accuracy, organization of results and reliability that is needed for conducting the simplest to the most complex searches. Our purpose is to take you on a journey into the world of Google search by describing the user interfaces, how Google works, and an assortment of search techniques, all the while sharing useful and effective tips, tricks and shortcuts for the sole purpose of performing better searches for better results.

The Google User Interface

Google's "free" and easy-to-use Internet search service begins with a very familiar user interface (or home page). Using a web browser such as Google Chrome®, Mozilla Firefox®, Internet Explorer®, or Safari®, the web address, www.Google.com, is entered as shown in Figure 1-1. By entering a keyword (or phrase) in the search box (section **1**) and clicking the "Google Search" button (section **2**), a basic user-initiated search can be requested. In addition to using the Google home page to search relevant results on the World Wide Web, users are also able to perform specific searches (i.e., You, Search, Images, Maps, Play, YouTube, News, Gmail, Documents, Calendar, and More) by clicking the links located at the top of the Google page (section **3**).

Figure 1-1. The Google User Interface

How Google Search Works

So, how does Google search work? You're definitely not the first to ask this question, and you won't be the last. We begin our explanation of how Google search works by dissecting the process into two distinct phases: 1) Google's web crawling, extraction and indexing process, and 2) Google's query process. The web crawling, extraction and indexing process, as illustrated in Figure 1-2, shows Google's automated web crawler, or a computer program (aka spider or Googlebot), browsing, extracting, and indexing (organizing) content from the World Wide Web by thousands of Google computers. The Googlebots begin by crawling (or searching) broad expanses of the Internet harvesting web pages and their links creating a list of links. The links are then organized, indexed and stored in Google databases.

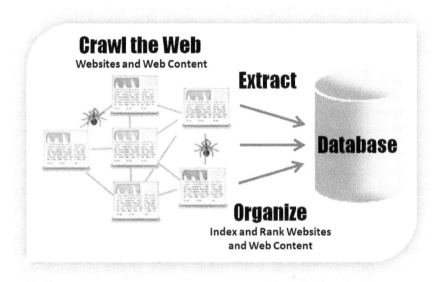

Figure 1-2. Web Crawling, Extraction, Organizing, and Indexing Process

The query process, as depicted in Figure 1-3, shows that as a query is submitted; the Google web servers immediately send the query to the index servers to determine the pages that contain the word(s) that match one or more query terms. The query is then sent to the doc servers where the stored content is retrieved, and the search results immediately returned to the Google user.

Figure 1-3. Query Process

Web Content and Google's PageRank® Algorithm

What makes Google search the most popular and widely used search application in the world? There are many factors, but one essential component is the creation of the ingenious **ranking** of web pages, links and content, known as PageRank®, developed by founders Lawrence Page and Sergey Brin. The PageRank algorithm ranks (or scores) web content with the greatest importance so that content is moved to the top of the user's search results allowing the Google web, index, and doc servers to return relevant and validated search results quickly. For example, a Google-search on [PageRank algorithm code] returns 32 million results, ranked with the most popular and important results appearing first in less than a second.

Currently, Stanford University holds the patent and Google has exclusive license rights to the proprietary PageRank algorithm. Although the exact number and type of parameters used in the ranking algorithm (originally dubbed "Backrub") is closely guarded, Google's website mentions that there are more than 200. To gain a better perspective, we peek under the hood, so to speak, by reading an important published paper (by Brin & Page, 1998) detailing the page ranking formula, when Google was still a university project. The formula for calculating PageRank and the explanation of its parameters is shown in Table 1, below.

$$PR(A) = (1-d) + d \left(PR(T1)/C(T1) + \ldots + PR(Tn)/C(Tn) \right)$$

Where PR(A) is the PageRank of Page A.
D is a dampening factor. Nominally this is set to 0.85.
PR(T1) is the PageRank of a site pointing to Page A.
C(T1) is the number of links off that page.
PR(Tn) /C(Tn) means we do that for each page pointing to Page A.

Source:
The Anatomy of a Large-Scale Hypertextual Web Search Engine, by Sergey Brin and Lawrence Page, http://www-db.stanford.edu/~backrub/google.html

Table 1. Formula for calculating PageRank
by Sergey Brin and Lawrence Page (1998)

An essential feature of Google's ranking algorithm applies greater importance to web content that contains page links from other pages. The algorithm also places greater importance to web content when it contains important links so that any links to other web pages also, by inheritance, become important.

In their in-depth and landmark papers, **PageRank Uncovered**, written by Chris Ridings and Mike Shishigin, and **How Google Ranks Web Pages** by Brian White, the basic features of Google's proprietary PageRank algorithm and how it ranks web content follows.

1. Find web content matching the keywords of the search.
2. Using the PageRank algorithm and its more than one hundred parameters, web content is ranked.
3. Compute the ranks once each month.
4. Return a list of the relevant pages using the current month's rankings.

Introducing Google's Hummingbird® Algorithm

The Google team is continually refining the parameters in their ranking algorithm, as well as the storage/index algorithm, to improve the speed and value associated with user searching.

As presented in the previous section, PageRank®, a brilliant algorithm used in Google search; Penguin, Panda, and other enhancements have been added as refinements. As recently as September 2013, a new and more enhanced algorithm called, Hummingbird®, replaced the PageRank algorithm, as well as the Penguin and Panda enhancements.

The Hummingbird® algorithm is a proprietary Google-developed algorithm used in the rewrite of the Google search engine. What is known about the Hummingbird algorithm (as stated by Google personnel) is that it supports general aspects of semantic discovery based on the known science of directed Knowledge Graphs. A few Hummingbird factors include:

- Spelling checks
- Autocomplete
- Search Methods
- Synonyms
- Query Understanding
- Google Instant
- Other factors

These semantic factors provide clues as to how the most relevant content are extracted from the index, prioritized, and displayed in a viewable list for Google users. Results are typically displayed on a desktop, laptop, tablet, or smartphone in 1/8th of a second.

Due to expectations for future enhancements to the Google search engine, it is a good idea to learn and become aware of the basics of using search keywords, and to continually follow a "planned" search strategy for each particular project in your areas of interest. Figure 1-4, below, depicts the Google search timeline.

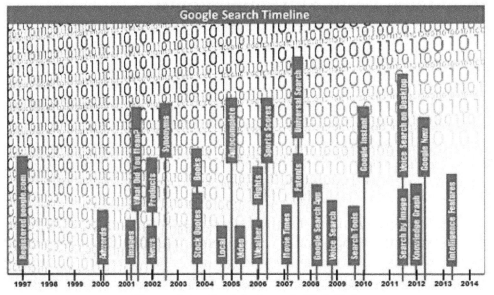

Figure 1-4. Google Search Timeline

Better Searches = Better Results

For anyone using Google, the importance of conducting successful searches is not only important; it may be an essential activity in conducting effective research required by your job. Because the Google search engine adheres to rules and processes the built-in algorithm makes every attempt to interpret your search requests while delivering the "best" results possible; in the end, the derived results are only as good as the search terms provided.

While many believe that conducting a "good" search is an exact science; the truth is that a successful search is more an art than anything else. The highest quality searches often require more than a single attempt at searching for something; consisting of a systematic, or iterative, process of refinement and sifting through results.

Becoming an effective and savvy Google searcher begins with understanding the objectives for the search, learning a few basic rules on how Google search works, and applying simple tips, tricks and shortcuts. To alleviate the challenges of finding the right combination of keywords, phrases and operators, a successful Google search should start with the development of a plan with details about the search. A detailed search plan is a necessary first step in conducting successful searches. The tips and techniques presented in Chapter 2 include a ten step approach for achieving better searches and better results for greater success.

> The highest quality searches often require a systematic, or iterative, process of refinement and sifting through results.

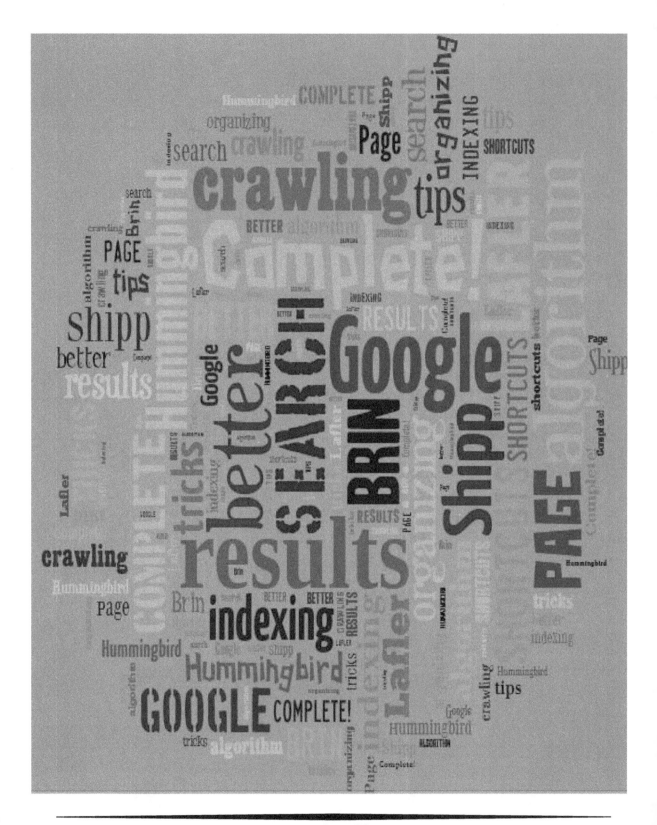

~ Chapter 2 ~

Planning Your Search

Planning Your Search

If you've never used the Google search tool, then you'll soon learn what all the excitement is about. And, if you're one of the billions of users who have then you know first-hand how simple and easy-to-use the search tool is. As a result of its ease-of-use, Google search users are given tremendous power to search the vast corners of the Internet and its ever-growing content of websites, databases, data sources, publications, text, images and what appears to be an endless supply of content. In fact, Google's decision to design the search website as an easy-to-use tool has indirectly empowered the researcher within all of us.

No longer are we faced with having to conduct our research within the confines of library walls or at the stacks in our Universities, and Public or Private Libraries. Google search gives us access to practically any content anywhere and anytime providing a unique advantage that was unattainable less than two decades ago.

Even with the power and flexibility a Google search provides, it is not sufficient to expect to find everything you're looking for without first understanding the importance that a little planning and preparation provides. To ensure the desired search results, users should pay attention to the process of planning and preparation of the keywords most appropriate to the topic being searched. The tips and techniques in this chapter present a ten step approach highlighting the things that should be done to conduct successful searches.

> The smart researcher writes commonly used synonyms, terms and/or phrases for each topic being searched.

A Ten Step Approach to Planning Your Search

Finding the right search content is typically not achieved by accident. A simple search for information often starts with entering one or more keywords. If the search results aren't exactly what is wanted or expected, then a change to one or more of the keywords may help in producing the desired search results.

When a simple search does not yield what is wanted or needed, more advanced search techniques may be required, see Section III. This often involves using an iterative approach until the desired level of success is achieved, see Section II.

To assist with the search process, a search is generally improved when a plan is implemented to help identify the objectives for the search, along with the available information resources and techniques to be used. The planning process is an iterative one involving several key elements, as shown in Figure 2-1.

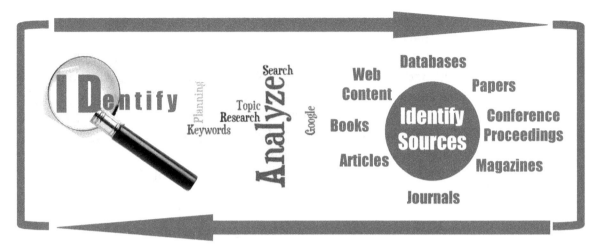

Figure 2-1. The Iterative Planning Process

Effective searches use a systematic, or iterative, approach to choosing the keywords, along with the other parameters, to be used. In these situations, a successful search may require breaking down the search topic(s) into subtopics which involve spending time understanding, planning and developing a strategy to improve the likelihood of success. By using a search planning form, like the one shown in Figure 2-2, researchers have a tool that can help improve their search results. Our ten step search approach is presented below.

1. Develop a search statement or sentence identifying what it is you want to search for using one or more keywords. Write out your search requirements completely, as shown in Figure 2-3.

2. Dissect the search statement you wrote into separate concepts or topics.

3. The smart researcher writes commonly used synonyms, terms and/or phrases for each concept or topic being searched. These synonyms, terms and phrases are referred to as your keywords. It is worth noting that being as specific as possible when deriving your keywords generally leads to better search results. Further, Google search will handle (using semantic analysis) subtle nuances of the language, as for example, "cactus vs. cacti". As you develop your keywords, keep these things in mind:

a. **Plurals** – Variations between the spelling of singular and plural words can impact search results. Examples of words with the same spelling for singular and plural include deer, buffalo, moose, fish, sheep, squid, and plankton, to name a few. Examples of words with spelling differences include woman vs. women; man vs. men; person vs. people; child vs. children; mouse vs. mice; cherry vs. cherries; sky vs. skies; message vs. messages; syllabus vs. syllabi; cactus vs. cacti; life vs. lives; index vs. indices; nucleus vs. nuclei; hero vs. heroes (or heros); calf vs. calves; leaf vs. leaves; hoof vs. hoofs (or hooves); elf vs. elfs (or elves); to name a few.

b. **Synonyms** – Examples include teenager vs. youth; senior citizen vs. elderly; big vs. large; small vs. little; fast vs. quick; smart vs. intelligent; speed vs. velocity.

c. **Abbreviations** – Examples include CA vs. California; BI vs. Business Intelligence; Dr vs. Doctor; PhD vs. Doctor; Prof. vs. Professor; Rev. vs. Reverend; US vs. United States; UK vs. United Kingdom; Interpol vs. International Police; HTML vs. Hyper-Text Markup Language; ANSI vs. American National Standards Institute.

d. **Spelling Variations** – Examples include color vs. colour; favorite vs. favourite; neighborhood vs. neighbourhood; paralyze vs. paralyse; matt vs. matte, organization vs. organization; database vs. data base.

e. **International Differences** – The world's most widely used system of measurements is the International Standards System which consists of kilogram, meters, kelvin, mole, ampere, candela and second. The basic physical quantities are: time, length, mass, electric current, temperature, amount of a substance and luminous intensity. Examples include weights and measurements such as U.S. standard vs. metric; Fahrenheit vs. Celsius; yard vs. meter;

f. **Terminology Variations** – Examples include programmer vs. coder; researcher vs. investigator; professional vs. skilled; employer vs. boss; student vs. pupil; relationship vs. interaction; Paramedic vs. health personnel; ingenious plot vs. clever plot.

4. Construct your search query using the synonyms, terms and/or phrases you developed in step #3, above. For phrases that are more than one word long, consider enclosing the phrase in quotation marks. To assist in constructing your search query, take advantage of Google's **AutoComplete** feature. AutoComplete displays helpful suggestions from the Google search engine using a drop-down list each time a synonym, term or phrase of a general nature is entered in the search box. The AutoComplete feature can be an indispensable method of discovering synonyms and other useful search terms related to what you're searching for. To take advantage of the AutoComplete feature for the browser you're using, you'll need to make sure that you have the AutoComplete feature turned on.

5. Avoid using any keywords that do not describe your topic in some way.

6. Apply Boolean logic such as AND, OR, and NOT to the keywords in your search query.

7. Begin your search narrowly and expand the search horizon iteratively. For example, begin by using a narrow Subject search, and then expand to a Title search, and then to a document text search for an expanded search horizon.

8. Use Google's search engine with subject references to access:
   a. Websites and web content
   b. Books, electronic books and other reliable resources
   c. Images
   d. Databases
   e. Journals
   f. Encyclopedias

9. Review search results addressing situations with too few or too many results, see Chapter 7 for additional insights.

10. Use flexibility when altering your search query by controlling the use of vocabulary when applying additional keywords to achieve desired results.

Benefits of Using the Ten Step Search Approach

As was mentioned earlier, finding the right search results is not by accident. A search is generally improved when a plan is implemented to help identify the objectives for the search, along with the available information resources and techniques to be used. Effective searches use a systematic approach to choosing the keywords, often breaking down the search topic(s) into subtopics which involve spending time understanding, planning and developing a strategy to improve the likelihood of success. In the authors' experience using the ten step search approach provides for better searches and better results.

> Following the Ten Step Google search approach increases the likelihood of finding what you are looking for.

Search Planning Form

1. Define the topic and objectives for the search you want to conduct.

2. List the primary requirements associated with your search. Include special conditions, considerations, time periods, geographical regions, languages, prices, and other parameters.

   Requirement 1:

   Requirement 2:

   Requirement 3:

   Requirement 4:

3. List keywords, synonyms, terms and phrases for your search query.

Requirement 1	Requirement 2	Requirement 3	Requirement 4

4. Prepare your search using keywords, synonyms, phrases, requirements, logical and comparison operators, special operators, punctuation symbols, etc.

Figure 2-2. Search Planning Form

Search Planning Form

1. Define the topic and objectives for the search you want to conduct.

   Purchase a new Schmidt-Cassegrain telescope

2. List the primary requirements associated with your search. Include special conditions, considerations, time periods, geographical regions, languages, prices, and other parameters.

   Requirement 1:   *Schmidt-Cassegrain telescope*

   Requirement 2:   *Computerized "GoTo" Tracking*

   Requirement 3:   *Light, portable, affordable, Cost $200-$1,200*

   Requirement 4:   *High-quality Optics, 2 – 12 inches Diameter*

3. List keywords, synonyms, terms and phrases for your search query.

Requirement 1	Requirement 2	Requirement 3	Requirement 4
Schmidt-	Easy tracking	Light	High-quality
Cassegrain	Computerized	Portable	Good Optics
Telescope	$200-$1,200	Affordable	2 – 12 inches

4. Prepare your search using keywords, synonyms, phrases, requirements, logical & comparison operators, special operators, punctuation symbols, etc.

   Schmidt-Cassegrain Telescope with a cost between $200 and $1,200 and diameter between 2 and 12 inches

Figure 2-3. Search Planning Form for Purchasing a Telescope

Section II

Search for Beginners

Process
Indexing
Google
PageRank
Search
techniques
Humming
results
algorithm
Complete
better
Lafler
shortcuts
Brin Page
tips
Web
planning
Organizing
Shipp
hummingbird
Crawling
search
Extraction
process
query

~ Chapter 3 ~

Basic Search Tips, Tricks and Shortcuts for Beginners

Basic Search Tips, Tricks and Shortcuts

Google provides incredible power to help you find what you want, whenever needed. A Google search query supports a maximum of 32 keywords enabling fully qualified searches for finding exactly what is wanted. Google search queries are not case sensitive meaning any typed letters, whether entered as uppercase, lowercase, or any combination of both are treated as lowercase characters. Table 3-1 presents a number of tips to consider in constructing searches.

Tip	Description
Keep it Short	Limit the number of search keywords specified for greater accuracy in the generation of search results.
Be Specific	When entering your search, be as specific as possible. Avoid generic (or vague) references when entering search keywords.
Use Quotes	Group compound words and phrases together, and search the words in the exact order specified.
Case Insensitive	Google search queries are not case sensitive so a search for Telescope finds content containing telescope, Telescope and TELESCOPE.
Word stem	Google automatically attaches suffixes to words which can greatly increase results. For example, specifying the search phrase *diet advice* will find results for dietary, dietician, diety, diet foods, diet pills, and diet plans; advice & relationships, advice center, and advice column; to list a few. **Note:** To turn word stemming off in a search, specify quotes around the search phrase or insert a + sign before the word.
Stopword	Common words that Google search typically ignores in a search include: a, about, above, after, an, and, are, as, before, below, between, both, could, down, each, etc, for, from, he, how, I, in, into, is, it, me, more, most, my, no, nor, not, of, off, on, or, she, should, so, some, such, that, the, their, there, this, to, too, under, until, up, very, was, were, what, when, where, who, will, with, would, www. **Note:** To force Google to recognize and use a stopword in a search, use quotes around the phrase or a + sign before the word.

Table 3-1. Basic Search Tips

Tip	Description
Wildcard (*)	The asterisk "*" (or wildcard) is used as a placeholder for unknown and/or partly known keywords.
Diacritic Marks	Searches for content that contain one or more diacritic marks or accent marks to assist with the pronunciation, sound or pitch of special characters in a language may require the appropriate language supported keyboard. Examples of words containing diacritic marks include café, résumé, jalapeño, exposé, and fiancée to name just a few. **Note:** Google searches return results containing words with and without accent marks.
AND	The AND (in all CAPS) is the default logical operator that Google uses between two or more keywords to search web content, and is therefore not required. Specifying 'and' (in lowercase) is treated as a stopword and is ignored in the search.
OR \<or\> |	The OR (in all CAPS) tells Google to search one of several keywords. The pipe symbol (|) can be substituted for the OR. **Note:** Specifying an "or" (NOT in caps) is treated as a stopword and ignored in the search.
– (Minus sign)	A word not wanted in a search query can be excluded by specifying a – (minus sign) before the word. **Note:** A blank space should precede a – (minus sign) to avoid confusing it with a hyphenated word.
Excluding Words	More than one word can be excluded from your search query by specifying a – (minus sign) before each keyword.
Specific Website	Google can be instructed to conduct all searches and produce search results from a specific website using the SITE: command.
Computations	Google can perform basic arithmetic computations.

Table 3-1. Basic Search Tips (continued)

A Google search query supports a maximum of 32 keywords enabling any search to be fully qualified for finding real value.

Sample Searches and the Range of Results

The range of results from a search depends on the keywords that are specified. To illustrate this point, a variety of search queries for the phrase, *Hubble Space Telescope* is specified, as illustrated in Table 3-2. As can be seen in the Results column, the specified search keywords and techniques used directly affects the number of results received. The use or non-use of quotes, the Boolean operators used, the specification and order of parentheses, and the use of other techniques affects a search and the results received. Consequently, it is essential to carefully plan your search queries by constructing effective search keywords, synonyms, and/or phrases.

Google Search	Results	Search Strategies
hubble space telescope	36.7 million	Default Boolean AND search.
"hubble space telescope"	2.76 million	Phrase search.
"hubble space" telescope	6.11 million	Partial phrase search.
hubble "space telescope"	14.3 million	Partial phrase search.
hubble AND space AND telescope	25 million	Adding Boolean AND search between each keyword.
hubble OR space OR telescope	746 million	Optional Boolean OR.
hubble | space | telescope	645 million	Optional Boolean | (OR).
hubble AND space OR telescope	65.4 million	Combination of Boolean AND and OR search.
hubble (space OR telescope)	32.2 million	Using parentheses with Boolean OR.
(hubble space) telescope	36.9 million	Using parentheses in search keywords.
hubble (space telescope)	37 million	Using parentheses in search keywords.
hubble +space +telescope	19	Connecting words with + signs.
hubble space +telescope	27	Connecting words with + sign.

Table 3-2. Sample Searches and the Range of Results

Basic Search

Basic Search Example

Example: **Being specific when searching for content.**
Search: **[hubble space telescope]**
Results: **18.5 million results in 0.64 seconds.**

Google | hubble space telescope | 🎤 | 🔍

Web   Images   News   Videos   Books   More ▾   Search tools

About 18,500,000 results (0.64 seconds)

Hubble Site - Out of the ordinary...out of this world.
hubblesite.org/ ▾ Hubble Space Telescope ▾
The Webb Space Telescope, Hubble's successor, will see in infrared, the light
emitted by the farthest objects we can detect. Learn about Webb, its technology, ...
Gallery - Picture Album - Wallpaper - The Telescope

Hubble Space Telescope - Wikipedia, the free encyclopedia
en.wikipedia.org/wiki/Hubble_Space_Telescope ▾ Wikipedia ▾
The **Hubble Space Telescope (HST)** is a space telescope that was carried into orbit
by a Space Shuttle in 1990 and remains in operation. A 2.4-meter (7.9 ft) ...
James Webb Space Telescope - Edwin Hubble - Hubble Deep Field - STS-31

News for **hubble space telescope**

Hubble Madness Puts Images Taken by **Hubble
Space Telescope** in Competition
Wall Street Journal - 17 hours ago
An online game created by scientists shows two images taken by
the **Hubble Space Telescope** at a time and asks the public to vote
on the best ...

Hubble spots comet heading towards Mars, spewing **space** dust
Sydney Morning Herald - by Deborah Netburn - 3 days ago

Huge 'El Gordo' galaxy cluster packs mass of 3 quadrillion suns
Fox News - 13 hours ago

More news for **hubble space telescope**

Hubble Space Telescope | NASA
www.nasa.gov/mission_pages/**hubble**/main/ ▾ NASA ▾
Mar 8, 2014 - Breathtaking photos and science-changing discoveries from over 20
years of exploration.

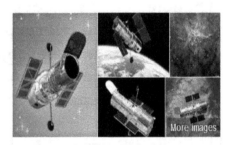

Hubble Space Telescope

Follow

The Hubble Space Telescope is a space telescope that was carried
into orbit by a Space Shuttle in 1990 and remains in operation.
Wikipedia

Orbit height: 347 miles (559 km)
Launch date: April 24, 1990
Speed on orbit: 4.66 miles/s (7.5 km/s)
Power: 2,800 watts
Cost: 2.5 billion USD

Recent posts

WE HAVE A WINNER. Victor in the 2014 Hubble
Madness Tournament, with 64 percent of the
public vote, is the Pillar in the Carina Nebula!
The image captures ... 3 hours ago

Feedback

Example: Using quotes to search for content.
Search: ["hubble space telescope"]
Results: 1.75 million results in 0.60 seconds.

Google | "hubble space telescope" | 🎤 | 🔍

Web   Images   News   Videos   Books   More ▾   Search tools

About 1,750,000 results (0.60 seconds)

HubbleSite - Out of the ordinary...out of this world.
hubblesite.org/ ▾ Hubble Space Telescope ▾
News center, gallery, discoveries, sci-tech, fun and games, and reference desk.
Gallery - Picture Album - Wallpaper - The Telescope

HubbleSite - The Telescope
hubblesite.org/the_telescope/ ▾ Hubble Space Telescope ▾
How Hubble works: its past, present and future; and the people behind it. The
Telescope - Hubble Essentials - Nuts & Bolts - Hand-Held Hubble - Team Hubble.

News for **"hubble space telescope"**

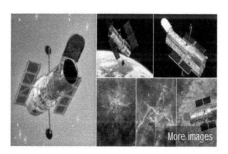

 Hubble Madness Puts Images Taken by **Hubble
Space Telescope** in Competition
Wall Street Journal - 1 day ago
An online game created by scientists shows two images taken by
the **Hubble Space Telescope** at a time and asks the public to vote
on the best ...

Hubble spots comet heading towards Mars, spewing space dust
Sydney Morning Herald - by Deborah Netburn - 4 days ago

Hubble spots comet heading toward Mars, spewing space dust
Los Angeles Times - by Deborah Netburn - 6 days ago

More news for **"hubble space telescope"**

Hubble Space Telescope - Wikipedia, the free encyclopedia
en.wikipedia.org/wiki/Hubble_Space_Telescope ▾ Wikipedia ▾
The **Hubble Space Telescope** (HST) is a space telescope that was carried into orbit
by a Space Shuttle in 1990 and remains in operation. A 2.4-meter (7.9 ft) ...
James Webb Space Telescope - Edwin Hubble - Hubble Deep Field - STS-31

Hubble Space Telescope

Follow

The Hubble Space Telescope is a space telescope that was carried
into orbit by a Space Shuttle in 1990 and remains in operation.
Wikipedia

Orbit height: 347 miles (559 km)
Launch date: April 24, 1990
Speed on orbit: 4.66 miles/s (7.5 km/s)
Power: 2,800 watts
Cost: 2.5 billion USD

Recent posts

 WE HAVE A WINNER. Victor in the 2014 Hubble
Madness Tournament, with 64 percent of the
public vote, is the Pillar in the Carina Nebula!
The image captures ... Apr 7, 2014

Example: **Producing case insensitive search results.**
Search: **[telescope]**
Results: **14.7 million results in 0.60 seconds.**

Google | telescope | 🎤 🔍

Web   Shopping   Images   Videos   Maps   More ▾   Search tools

About 14,700,000 results (0.60 seconds)

Telescopes at Amazon.com
Ad www.amazon.com/ ▾
Buy **telescopes** at Amazon! Free Shipping on Qualified Orders.

Telescopes Super Sale - **Telescopes**.com
Ad www.telescopes.com/ ▾
Shop **Telescopes** in Top Brands & All Models. Lowest Prices & Free S/H!
Telescopes Super Sale - Kids Telescopes - Celestron Telescopes

Orion **Telescopes** & Binoculars: Official Site - **Telescope**.com
www.telescope.com/ ▾ Orion Telescopes & Binoculars ▾
The friendly experts at Orion will help you choose the right **telescope**, binoculars, or
accessories. Same-day shipping. 100% satisfaction guarantee!
Telescopes - Dobsonian Telescopes - Accessories - Refractor Telescopes

Telescopes and **Telescope** Accessories from Celestron, Mea...
www.telescopes.com/ ▾
All **telescopes** and **telescope** accessories on sale every day at Telescopes.com.
Shop our quality collection of reflecting, refracting catadoptric telescopes from ...

News for **telescope**

Hints of Dark Matter Seen At Milky Way's Center By
NASA's Fermi Space **Telescope** (VIDEO)
Huffington Post - 1 day ago
In the new study, researchers used data from NASA's Fermi
Gamma-ray Space **Telescope** to make maps of the Milky Way's
center in ...

Excessive Gamma Rays at Milky Way's Center Hint at Dark Matter
Voice of America (blog) - 4 days ago

More news for **telescope**

Shop for **telescope** on Google   Sponsored ⓘ

Celestron   Celestron   Celestron   Celestron
PowerSeeker...   AstroMaster 7...   AstroMaster 1...   Telescopes C...
$165.50 $108.98 $159.98 $8,999.00
Rakuten.c...   Rakuten.c...   Hayneedle   OpticsPla...
                                                         ⬥ Special offer

Orion StarBlast   Orion StarMax   Sky-Watcher   Celestron
6 Astro Refle...   90mm TableT...   12" Dobsonia...   Telescopes P...
$289.99 $189.99 $999.00 $134.99
telescope.com   telescope.com   Telescopes c...   OpticsPla...
                                                         ⬥ Special offer

Ads ⓘ

Celestron **Telescopes** Sale
www.opticsplanet.com/CelestronTelescope ▾
4.6 ★★★★☆ rating for opticsplanet.com
Up to 60% Off Celestron **Telescopes**.
Full Line. Free S&H. Life Warranty!

Telescopes on Sale
www.hayneedle.com/Telescopes ▾
4.6 ★★★★☆ rating for hayneedle.com
Find More Options & Savings for
You at Hayneedle, 30-50% Off Sale

Example: **Ignoring stopwords in searches.**

Search: **[buying a used car]**

Results: **353 million results in 0.47 seconds.**

 buying a used car 🎤 🔍

Web   Videos   Shopping   Images   News   More ▾   Search tools

About 353,000,000 results (0.47 seconds)

AutoTrader.com® - Find a **Used** Sedan in Your Area   ⓘ
Ad www.**autotrader**.com/ ▾
Search & Compare Local Listings.
AutoTrader.com has 246,977 followers on Google+
Find Local Cars - Compare Used Models

Car Buying Tips - Edmunds.com
Ad www.edmunds.com/ ▾
Car at Edmunds.com Search New Car Listings Nearby
Edmunds.com has 1,692,741 followers on Google+
New Car Quotes - Price Promise Listings

Used Cars From $100/Month - **Auto**List.com
Ad www.autolist.com/**UsedCars** ▾
Search From 272,300+ Local **Cars**. Compare and Get the Best Deal Now!

10 Steps to **Buying a Used Car** - Edmunds.com ✅
 www.edmunds.com/car-buying/10-steps-to-buyin... ▾ Edmunds.com ▾
by Philip Reed - in 133 Google+ circles
Nov 8, 2002 - The following steps will tell you how to locate, price and
negotiate to **buy** the **used car** you want. If you don't yet know what car to **buy**,
read "10 ...
How to Get a Used Car Bargain - Program Cars, Rental Cars ... - Used Car
Inventory

Buying a Used Car | Consumer Information ✅
https://www.consumer.ftc.gov/.../0055-buying... ▾ Federal Trade Commission ▾
Before you start shopping for a **used car**, do some homework. It may save you

Ads ⓘ

CARFAX® **Cars** For Sale
www.carfax.com/Cars_For_Sale ▾
4.7 ★★★★★ rating for carfax.com
Find The Right **Car** With The Right
History w/ CARFAX Used Car Listings

Certified Pre-Owned **Cars**
vw.worldautocertified.com/ ▾
View Current Special VW Offers.
Locate Your Nearest Dealer Now.

Used Cars For Sale
www.mbsd.com/ ▾
Huge Selection & Amazing Prices.
Buy Your Next Used Car Here

Top Dollar Paid - 2 Hours
www.webuycars.com/CarBuyers ▾
(855) 990-3125
Get A Quote Right Now - No Waiting.
Like New, Wrecked or Not Running

Official Kelley Blue Book
www.kbb.com/ ▾
Research Used Car Values, Specs and
Read Reviews at Kelley Blue Book®.

Basic Search

Basic Search Example

Example: **Recognizing stopwords in searches.**
Search: **[buying +a used car]**
Results: **5,170 results in 0.49 seconds.**

Google   buying +a used car   🎤 🔍

Web   Videos   Shopping   Images   News   More ▾   Search tools

About 5,170 results (0.49 seconds)

AutoTrader.com® - Find a **Used** Sedan in Your Area   ⓘ   Ads ⓘ
[Ad] www.**autotrader**.com/ ▾
Search & Compare Local Listings.   CARFAX® **Cars** For Sale
AutoTrader.com has 246,977 followers on Google+   www.carfax.com/Cars_For_Sale ▾
Find Local Cars - Compare Used Models   CARFAX Now Offers Used Car Listings
                                                                   Including **Vehicle** History Reports!

How To Buy A **Car** - Edmunds.com
[Ad] www.**edmunds**.com/ ▾   **Used Cars** From $100/Month
Auto Buying Tips, Reviews, Pricing Get Local Dealer Invoice Prices. www.autolist.com/UsedCars ▾
Edmunds.com has 1,692,741 followers on Google+   Search From 272,300+ Local Cars.
New Car Quotes - Price Promise Listings   Compare and Get the Best Deal Now!

10 Steps to **Buying a Used Car** - Edmunds.com   San Diego Pre-Owned **Cars**
www.edmunds.com/**car-buying**/10-steps-to-buyin... ▾ Edmunds.com ▾ www.mossynissan.com/ ▾
by Philip Reed - in 133 Google+ circles   (866) 737-1054
Nov 8, 2002 - The following steps will tell you how to locate, price and   Mossy Nissan's Huge Selection
negotiate to buy the used car you want. If you don't yet know what car to buy, Over 400 used cars in stock
read "10 ...
How to Get a Used Car Bargain - Program Cars, Rental Cars ... - Used Car
Inventory   How To Buy A **Car**
                                                                   www.howtobuyacarinfo.com/ ▾
10 Steps To **Buying A Used Car** - Kelley Blue Book   For complete guidance on **buying** a
www.kbb.com/car.../car-buying/step-1-find-out-how-... ▾ Kelley Blue Book ▾ new car or used car visit our site
Make car buying a pleasant experience by read and use 10 Steps To **Buying** a Used
Car advice article to get the best deal on your next used car purchase.   Certified Pre-Owned **Cars**
                                                                   vw.world**auto**certified.com/ ▾
How to **Buy a Used** a Car | The Art of Manliness   View Current Special VW Offers.
www.artofmanliness.com/2010/04/11/how-to-**buy-a-used-car**/ ▾   Locate Your Nearest Dealer Now.

                                                                   See your ad here »

Example: **Searching content containing diacritic marks.**

Search: **[winning résumés]**

Results: **97.9 million results in 0.39 seconds.**

Google | winning résumés | 🔍

Web   Images   News   Shopping   Videos   More ⏷   Search tools

About 97,900,000 results (0.39 seconds)

Ten Tips for an Interview **Winning Resume** - Job Searching
jobsearch.about.com › Careers › Job Searching › Resumes ▾ About.com ▾
Start by including a well-written resume cover letter with the resume. Then, follow
these resume tips to create an interview **winning resume** that is head and ...

Images for **winning résumés**   Report images

More images for **winning résumés**

5 do's and don'ts for building a **winning resume** - USA Today
www.usatoday.com/story/news/.../09/...resume/2875465/ ▾ USA Today ▾
Sep 27, 2013 - A great **resume** can be a game changer for you in your job hunt. In
the 15 seconds (if you're lucky) a recruiter will peruse it, you can jump to the ...

Anatomy of a **Winning Resume** [INFOGRAPHIC] - Mashable
mashable.com/2013/02/.../**winning-resume**-infographi... ▾ Mashable ▾
by Anita Li
Feb 17, 2013 - Searching for jobs is a daunting task for many, so it's
imperative your **resume** is in tip-top shape. With 25% of human-resources
managers ...

William & Mary - 15 Tips for Writing **Winning Résumés**
www.wm.edu/.../**resumes**1/**winningresume**ti... ▾ College of William and Mary ▾
Here are 15 tips to help you not only tackle the task, but also write a **winning
resume**;. 1. Determine your job search objective prior to writing the resume;.

Writing a **Winning Resume** | CAA
alumni.berkeley.edu/.../**resumes**/writin... ▾ University of California, Berkeley ▾

Example: **Searching content with a wildcard.**

Search: **[hubble space telescope *]**

Results: **12.2 million results in 0.57 seconds.**

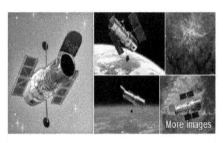

Google   hubble space telescope *

Web   Images   News   Videos   Shopping   More ▾   Search tools

About 12,200,000 results (0.57 seconds)

ESA/Hubble
www.spacetelescope.org/ ▾
Media advisory: Science with the Hubble Space Telescope IV conference. 24
January 2014. January 2014 issue of ESA/Hubble Science Newsletter now ...

STScI Office of Public Outreach
outreachoffice.stsci.edu/ ▾ Space Telescope Science Institute ▾
... Education and Public Outreach (E/PO) activities for NASA's **Hubble Space
Telescope** (HST) and the upcoming James Webb Space Telescope (JWST).

Hubble Space Telescope - Wikipedia, the free encyclopedia
en.wikipedia.org/wiki/**Hubble_Space_Telescope** ▾ Wikipedia ▾
The **Hubble Space Telescope** (HST) is a space telescope that was carried into orbit
by a Space Shuttle in 1990 and remains in operation. A 2.4-meter (7.9 ft) ...
James Webb Space Telescope - Edwin Hubble - Hubble Deep Field - STS-31

HubbleSite - Out of the ordinary...out of this world.
hubblesite.org/ ▾ Hubble Space Telescope ▾
The Webb **Space Telescope, Hubble's** successor, will see in infrared, the light
emitted by the farthest objects we can detect. Learn about Webb, its technology, ...
Gallery - Picture Album - Wallpaper - The Telescope

HubbleSite - NewsCenter
hubblesite.org/newscenter/ ▾ Hubble Space Telescope ▾
... of every **Hubble Space Telescope news** release and its supporting materials, ...
The **Hubble Space Telescope is a mission** of the NASA Origins Program.

HubbleSite - Picture Album
hubblesite.org/gallery/album/ ▾ Hubble Space Telescope ▾
... by Hubble scientists and you. Hubble Heritage Dedicated to finding and
publicizing the most visually appealing images from the **Hubble Space Telescope.**

HubbleSite - NewsCenter - Entire Collection
hubblesite.org/newscenter/archive ▾ Hubble Space Telescope ▾
20+ items - Search all of HubbleSite. HubbleSite · HOME · NEWSCENTER ..

More images

Hubble Space Telescope

The Hubble Space Telescope is a space telescope that was carried
into orbit by a Space Shuttle in 1990 and remains in operation.
Wikipedia

Orbit height: 347 miles (559 km)

Launch date: April 24, 1990

Speed on orbit: 4.66 miles/s (7.5 km/s)

Power: 2,800 watts

Cost: 2.5 billion USD

Feedback

Example: **Searching content with implied "AND" logic.**

Search: **[hubble space telescope]**

Results: **18.5 million results in 0.64 seconds.**

Google   hubble space telescope

Web   Images   News   Videos   Books   More ▾   Search tools

About 18,500,000 results (0.64 seconds)

HubbleSite - Out of the ordinary...out of this world.
hubblesite.org/ ▾ Hubble Space Telescope ▾
The Webb **Space Telescope**, **Hubble**'s successor, will see in infrared, the light
emitted by the farthest objects we can detect. Learn about Webb, its technology, ...
Gallery - Picture Album - Wallpaper - The Telescope

Hubble Space Telescope - Wikipedia, the free encyclopedia
en.wikipedia.org/wiki/**Hubble_Space_Telescope** ▾ Wikipedia ▾
The **Hubble Space Telescope** (HST) is a space telescope that was carried into orbit
by a Space Shuttle in 1990 and remains in operation. A 2.4-meter (7.9 ft) ...
James Webb Space Telescope - Edwin Hubble - Hubble Deep Field - STS-31

News for **hubble space telescope**

Hubble Madness Puts Images Taken by **Hubble**
Space Telescope in Competition
Wall Street Journal - 17 hours ago
An online game created by scientists shows two images taken by
the **Hubble Space Telescope** at a time and asks the public to vote
on the best ...

Hubble spots comet heading towards Mars, spewing **space** dust
Sydney Morning Herald - by Deborah Netburn - 3 days ago

Huge 'El Gordo' galaxy cluster packs mass of 3 quadrillion suns
Fox News - 13 hours ago

More news for **hubble space telescope**

Hubble Space Telescope | NASA
www.nasa.gov/mission_pages/**hubble**/main/ ▾ NASA ▾
Mar 8, 2014 - Breathtaking photos and science-changing discoveries from over 20
years of exploration.

More images

Hubble Space Telescope

Follow

The Hubble Space Telescope is a space telescope that was carried
into orbit by a Space Shuttle in 1990 and remains in operation.
Wikipedia

Orbit height: 347 miles (559 km)

Launch date: April 24, 1990

Speed on orbit: 4.66 miles/s (7.5 km/s)

Power: 2,800 watts

Cost: 2.5 billion USD

Recent posts

WE HAVE A WINNER. Victor in the 2014 Hubble
Madness Tournament, with 64 percent of the
public vote, is the Pillar in the Carina Nebula!
The image captures ... 9 hours ago

Feedback

Example: **Searching content with "ANDed" logic.**
Search: **[hubble AND space AND telescope]**
Results: **Almost 11 million results in 0.55 seconds.**

Google | hubble AND space AND telescope   🎤   🔍

Web   News   Videos   Images   Shopping   More ▾   Search tools

About 10,900,000 results (0.55 seconds)

Hubble Site - Out of the ordinary...out of this world.
hubblesite.org/ ▾ Hubble Space Telescope ▾
The Webb **Space Telescope**, **Hubble's** successor, will see in infrared, the light
emitted by the farthest objects we can detect. Learn about Webb, its technology, ...
Gallery - Picture Album - Wallpaper - The Telescope

Hubble Site - Gallery
hubblesite.org/gallery/ ▾ Hubble Space Telescope ▾
At the official online home of NASA's **Hubble Space Telescope** exists a gallery of the
best pictures that the Hubble has taken.

Hubble Site - The **Telescope**
hubblesite.org/the_telescope/ ▾ Hubble Space Telescope ▾
How **Hubble** works; its past, present and future; and the people behind it. ... The
Webb **Telescope** NASA's Next **Space Telescope** Advanced technology drives ...

Hubble Space Telescope - Wikipedia, the free encyclopedia
en.wikipedia.org/wiki/**Hubble_Space_Telescope** ▾ Wikipedia ▾
The **Hubble Space Telescope** (HST) is a space telescope that was carried into orbit
by a Space Shuttle in 1990 and remains in operation. A 2.4-meter (7.9 ft) ...
James Webb Space Telescope - Edwin Hubble - Hubble Deep Field - STS-31

News for **hubble AND space AND telescope**

 Hubble Madness Puts Images Taken by **Hubble
Space Telescope** in Competition
Wall Street Journal - 17 hours ago
An online game created by scientists shows two images taken by
the **Hubble Space Telescope** at a time and asks the public to vote
on the best ...

Hubble spots comet heading towards Mars, spewing **space** dust
Sydney Morning Herald - by Deborah Netburn - 3 days ago

Hubble spots comet heading toward Mars, spewing **space** dust
Los Angeles Times - by Deborah Netburn - 5 days ago

Example: **Searching content with "and-ed" logic.**

Search: **[hubble and space and telescope]**

Results: **Almost 11 million results in 0.52 seconds.**

Google | hubble and space and telescope   🎤 🔍

Web   News   Videos   Images   Shopping   More ▾   Search tools

About 10,900,000 results (0.52 seconds)

Hubble Site - Out of the ordinary...out of this world.
hubblesite.org/ ▾ Hubble Space Telescope ▾
The Webb **Space Telescope**, **Hubble**'s successor, will see in infrared, the light
emitted by the farthest objects we can detect. Learn about Webb, its technology, ...
Gallery - Picture Album - Wallpaper - The Telescope

Hubble Site - Gallery
hubblesite.org/gallery/ ▾ Hubble Space Telescope ▾
At the official online home of NASA's **Hubble Space Telescope** exists a gallery of the
best pictures that the Hubble has taken.

Hubble Site - The **Telescope**
hubblesite.org/the_telescope/ ▾ Hubble Space Telescope ▾
How **Hubble** works; its past, present and future; and the people behind it. ... The
Webb **Telescope** NASA's Next **Space Telescope** Advanced technology drives ...

Hubble Space Telescope - Wikipedia, the free encyclopedia
en.wikipedia.org/wiki/**Hubble_Space_Telescope** ▾ Wikipedia ▾
The **Hubble Space Telescope** (HST) is a space telescope that was carried into orbit
by a Space Shuttle in 1990 and remains in operation. A 2.4-meter (7.9 ft) ...
James Webb Space Telescope - Edwin Hubble - Hubble Deep Field - STS-31

News for **hubble and space and telescope**

 Hubble Madness Puts Images Taken by **Hubble
Space Telescope** in Competition
Wall Street Journal - 18 hours ago
An online game created by scientists shows two images taken by
the **Hubble Space Telescope** at a time and asks the public to vote
on the best ...

Hubble spots comet heading towards Mars, spewing **space** dust
Sydney Morning Herald - by Deborah Netburn - 4 days ago

Hubble spots comet heading toward Mars, spewing **space** dust
Los Angeles Times - by Deborah Netburn - 5 days ago

Example: **Searching content with embedded "OR" logic.**
Search: **[hubble OR space OR telescope]**
Results: **715 million results in 0.63 seconds.**

Google | hubble OR space OR telescope

Web   Images   Videos   News   Books   More ▾   Search tools

About 715,000,000 results (0.63 seconds)

HubbleSite - Out of the ordinary...out of this world.
hubblesite.org/ ▾ Hubble Space Telescope ▾
The Webb **Space Telescope**, **Hubble's** successor, will see in infrared, the light
emitted by the farthest objects we can detect. Learn about Webb, its technology, ...
Gallery - Picture Album - Wallpaper - The Telescope

Space and NASA News – Universe and Deep **Space** Informatio...
www.**space**.com/ ▾ space.com ▾
Get the latest outer **space** and science news, NASA information, watch **space** flight
videos at Space.com. ... NASA Seeks Partners to Save SOFIA Flying Telescope
Galaxy 'Serial Killer' Caught in the Act of ... **Hubble** eXtreme Deep Field (XDF).
Watch It Live - Space News - Image of the Day - Webcasts

News for **hubble OR space OR telescope**

Hubble Madness Puts Images Taken by **Hubble**
Space Telescope in Competition
Wall Street Journal - 17 hours ago
An online game created by scientists shows two images taken by
the **Hubble Space Telescope** at a time and asks the public to vote
on the best ...

The Horsehead Nebula, a red-hot game favourite. Source: Supplied
The Australian - 12 hours ago

More news for **hubble OR space OR telescope**

Hubble Space Telescope | NASA
www.nasa.gov/mission_pages/**hubble**/main/ ▾ NASA ▾
Mar 8, 2014 - Breathtaking photos and science-changing discoveries from over 20
years of exploration.

More images

Hubble Space Telescope

Follow

The Hubble Space Telescope is a space telescope that was carried
into orbit by a Space Shuttle in 1990 and remains in operation.
Wikipedia

Orbit height: 347 miles (559 km)

Launch date: April 24, 1990

Speed on orbit: 4.66 miles/s (7.5 km/s)

Power: 2,800 watts

Cost: 2.5 billion USD

Recent posts

WE HAVE A WINNER. Victor in the 2014 Hubble
Madness Tournament, with 64 percent of the
public vote, is the Pillar in the Carina Nebula!
The image captures ... 4 hours ago

Example: **Searching content with embedded "or" logic.**
Search: **[hubble or space or telescope]**
Results: **10.8 million results in 0.52 seconds.**

Google   hubble or space or telescope   🎤 🔍

Web   Images   Shopping   News   Videos   More ▾   Search tools

About 10,800,000 results (0.52 seconds)

Images for **hubble or space or telescope**   Report images

More images for **hubble or space or telescope**

Hubble Site - Out of the ordinary...out of this world.
hubblesite.org/ ▾ Hubble Space Telescope
The Webb **Space Telescope**, **Hubble's** successor, will see in infrared, the light
emitted by the farthest objects we can detect. Learn about Webb, its technology, ...
Gallery - Picture Album - Wallpaper - The Telescope

Hubble Site - Gallery
hubblesite.org/gallery/ ▾ Hubble Space Telescope ▾
At the official online home of NASA's **Hubble Space Telescope** exists a gallery of the
best pictures that the Hubble has taken.

Hubble Site - NewsCenter
hubblesite.org/newscenter/ ▾ Hubble Space Telescope ▾
NewsCenter is the complete collection of every **Hubble Space Telescope** news
release and its supporting materials, along with tools and resources designed to ...

Hubble Space Telescope - Wikipedia, the free encyclopedia
en.wikipedia.org/wiki/**Hubble_Space_Telescope** ▾ Wikipedia ▾
The **Hubble Space Telescope** (HST) is a space telescope that was carried into orbit
by a Space Shuttle in 1990 and remains in operation. A 2.4-meter (7.9 ft) ...
James Webb Space Telescope - Edwin Hubble - Hubble Deep Field - STS-31

Example: **Excluding keywords with a [-] (minus) sign.**

Search: **[hubble space telescope –microscope –apps]**

Results: **18.4 million results in 0.63 seconds.**

Google   hubble space telescope -microscope -apps   🎤

Web   Images   News   Videos   Books   More ▾   Search tools

About 18,400,000 results (0.63 seconds)

Hubble Space Telescope - Wikipedia, the free encyclopedia
en.wikipedia.org/wiki/**Hubble_Space_Telescope** ▾ Wikipedia ▾
The **Hubble Space Telescope** (HST) is a space telescope that was carried into orbit
by a Space Shuttle in 1990 and remains in operation. A 2.4-meter (7.9 ft) ...
James Webb Space Telescope - Edwin Hubble - Hubble Deep Field - STS-31

HubbleSite - The **Telescope**
hubblesite.org/the_telescope/ ▾ Hubble Space Telescope ▾
How **Hubble** works; its past, present and future; and the people behind it. ... The
Webb Telescope NASA's Next **Space Telescope** Advanced technology drives ...

HubbleSite - NewsCenter
hubblesite.org/newscenter/ ▾ Hubble Space Telescope ▾
NewsCenter is the complete collection of every **Hubble Space Telescope** news
release and its supporting materials, along with tools and resources designed to ...

News for **hubble space telescope -microscope -apps**

Hubble Madness Puts Images Taken by **Hubble Space
Telescope** in Competition
Wall Street Journal - 20 hours ago
Ernie Ostuno had two big hopes recently: victory for his Michigan teams in the March
Madness basketball competition and the conquest of the universe.

Hubble spots comet heading towards Mars, spewing **space** dust
Sydney Morning Herald - by Deborah Netburn - 3 days ago

More news for **hubble space telescope -microscope -apps**

HST - STScI
www.stsci.edu/hst/ ▾ Space Telescope Science Institute ▾
NASA and the Space Telescope Science Institute released the Cycle 22 Call for
Proposals for **Hubble Space Telescope** (HST) Observations and funding for ...

Example: **Combining more than one idea with AND.**

Search: **[("diet plan" OR "diet program") AND ("weight loss" OR "weight reduction")]**

Results: **21.6 million results in 0.27 seconds.**

Google | ("diet plan" OR "diet program") AND ("weight loss" OR "weight reduction") | 🎤 🔍

Web   Images   News   Shopping   Videos   More ▾   Search tools

About 21,600,000 results (0.27 seconds)

Diet Program That Works - Meal Replacement **Diet Plan**   ⓘ
Ad www.medifast1.com/ ▾
Tasty, Healthy & Proven **Weight Loss**
"No counting carbs, points, or calories." – US News
Medifast has 596 followers on Google+

$2.42 per Meal   Free Shipping Plan
Online Store   20,000 Doctors Recommend

15-Day **Weight Loss** Trial
Ad www.rxweightlossinfo.com/ ▾
A Treatment Option For Adults. Learn More At The Official Site.
Information Page - Patient Card *Terms Apply - Voucher Registration

Weight Loss Program - PremierFitnessCamp.com
Ad www.premierfitnesscamp.com/ ▾   (855) 840-0385
Change Your Life, Escape the Cold, & Lose Weight at Top CA Resort!
📍 2100 Costa Del Mar Road, Carlsbad, CA

The Biggest Loser 7-Day **Diet Plan** - Ladies' Home Journal ✅
www.lhj.com › ... › Weight Loss › Getting Started ▾ Ladies' Home Journal ▾
Just because you're not a contestant on the show doesn't mean you can't win your
own **weight-loss** battle at home. To help you get started, we asked The ...

Can you give a **diet plan** for quick **weight loss** in 7 days ... ✅
www.thehealthsite.com/.../can-you-give-a-**diet-plan**-for-quick-**weight-los**... ▾
Dec 9, 2013 - I've been trying to lose weight for a long time. Could you please give
me a diet to lose weight in 7 days? Losing weight is not a complex affair.

Ads

The Fresh Diet California
www.thefreshdiet.com/ ▾
3 Gourmet Meals + 2 Snacks Daily.
Cooked & Delivered Daily To You!

Fat Freezing San Diego
www.drbucko.com/ ▾
(855) 739-7040
Non-surgical fat removal.
Dedicated CoolSculpting staff.
📍 3655 Nobel Dr., Suite 100, San Diego

Jenny Craig® **Weight Loss**
www.jennycraig.com/ ▾
Kirstie is Down 10lbs.*Find Out How
She Did it By Joining Jenny Craig®

Nutrisystem® **Weight Loss**
www.nutrisystem.com/Lose-Weight ▾
(855) 662-1207
Slim Down Just In Time For Summer.
Free Jumpstart Week - Fast 5™!

Lose Twice the Weight...
www.ihmonline.com/ ▾
(619) 297-8640
in half the time with HMR!

Example #1 – Purchasing a New Telescope

Now that a few basic search tips and techniques have been illustrated, let's return to the example we developed in Chapter 2 on purchasing a new telescope. The objective is to translate the specifications that were collected on the planning form, as shown in Figure 3-1 to a search query that can be entered to produce results containing new telescopes, as shown in Figure 3-2.

Planning Form – Purchasing a New Telescope

1. Define the topic and objectives for the search you want to conduct.

    Purchase a new Schmidt-Cassegrain telescope

2. List the primary requirements associated with your search. Include special conditions, considerations, time periods, geographical regions, languages, prices, and other parameters.

   Requirement 1:   *Schmidt-Cassegrain telescope*

   Requirement 2:   *Computerized "GoTo" Tracking*

   Requirement 3:   *Light, portable, affordable, Cost $200-$1,200*

   Requirement 4:   *High-quality Optics, 2 – 12 inches Diameter*

3. List keywords, synonyms, terms and phrases for your search query.

Requirement 1	Requirement 2	Requirement 3	Requirement 4
Schmidt-	Easy tracking	Light	High-quality
Cassegrain	Computerized	Portable	Good Optics
Telescope	$200-$1,200	Affordable	2 – 12 inches

4. Prepare your search using keywords, synonyms, phrases, requirements, logical & comparison operators, special operators, punctuation symbols, etc.

    Schmidt-Cassegrain Telescope with a cost between $200 and $1,200 and diameter between 2 and 12 inches

Figure 3-1. Search Planning Form for Purchasing a New Telescope

Planning Form – Purchasing a New Telescope

1. Define the topic and objectives for the search you want to conduct.

   Purchase a new Schmidt-Cassegrain telescope

2. List the primary requirements associated with your search. Include special conditions, considerations, time periods, geographical regions, languages, prices, and other parameters.

   Requirement 1: *Schmidt-Cassegrain telescope*

   Requirement 2: *Computerized "GoTo" Tracking*

   Requirement 3: *Light, portable, affordable, Cost $200-$1,200*

   Requirement 4: *High-quality Optics, 2 – 12 inches Diameter*

3. List keywords, synonyms, terms and phrases for your search query.

Requirement 1	Requirement 2	Requirement 3	Requirement 4
Schmidt-Cassegrain Telescope	Easy tracking Computerized $200-$1,200	Light Portable Affordable	High-quality Good Optics 2 – 12 inches

4. Prepare your search using keywords, synonyms, phrases, requirements, logical & comparison operators, special operators, punctuation symbols, etc.

   [Schmidt-Cassegrain Telescope $200 . . $1,200 AND diameter 2 . . 12 inches]

Figure 3-2. Search Planning Form for Purchasing a New Telescope

Example: **Searching telescopes $200 – $1,200 with 2 – 12 inch diameter.**

Search: **[Schmidt-cassegrain telescope $200 . . $1,200 AND diameter 2 . . 12 inches]**

Results: **71 results in 0.60 seconds.**

Google | Schmidt-cassegrain telescope $200 . . $1,200 AND diameter 2 . . 12 inches

Web   Shopping   Images   Videos   News   More ▾   Search tools

71 results (0.60 seconds)

Shopping for a New Telescope: Meade vs. Celestron ...
www.telescopes.com/telescopes/meadevscelestrontelescopesarticle.cfm ▾
Words like Schmidt-Cassegrain telescopes and Dobsonian telescopes do not
sound ... Both companies offer entry level telescopes under $200. ... and the largest
aperture NexStar 8SE telescope is priced under $1200. ... the Meade LX200 ACF
telescopes come in 8-inch, 10-inch, 12-inch, 14 inch and even 16-inch models.
Missing: diameter

2013 Telescope Awards - Telescopes.com
www.telescopes.com/telescopes/telescopeawardsarticle.cfm ▾
Telescopes.com 2013 Telescopes Award Winners. ... The 10-, 12-, and 14-inch
models are all equipped with fast f/8 ACF optics that create wide, flat fields great ...
Missing: $1200 diameter

[PDF] **Buying the Best Telescope**
www.fvastro.org/beginners/BuyingBestTelescope.pdf ▾
The "6-inch" refers to the diameter of the main, or primary, mirror. ... Cassegrain or
Maksutov-Cassegrain telescopes offer 3½- to 5-inch (90- to 125-mm) ... fold a 48-
inch focal length into a tube no more than 12 inches long. ... Approximate prices:
$600 to $1,200 for a 3½- to 5-inch Maksutov- or Schmidt-Cassegrain telescope.

Orion Telescopes: Search Results on 'solar filter'
www.telescope.com/catalog/search.cmd?... ▾ Orion Telescopes & Binoculars ▾
Up to $25 $25 - $50 $50 - $75 $75 - $125 $125 - $200 $200 - $400 $1200 - $1600 ...
This filter fits 11" Schmidt-Cassegrain Telescopes. ... fits the Orion SkyQuest XT12
Dobsonian telescope and XX12 IntelliScope Truss Tube Dobsonian. .... This set of
two glass solar filters with an inside diameter of 4.30" fit Orion 20x80 ...

Orion Telescopes: Search Results on 'accessories'
www.telescope.com/.../search.cmd?... ▾ Orion Telescopes & Binoculars ▾
... $200 $200 - $400 $400 - $600 $600 - $800 $800 - $1200 $1200 - $1600 1600 -
$2400 Over $2400 ... Up to 12mm 12mm - 20mm 13mm - 20mm Over 20mm. Barrel
diameter: ..... Tele Vue Standard Schmidt-Cassegrain Telescope Adapter ..... Made
of rugged black-anodized aluminum, this big 2 inch "nosepiece" is ...

Example #2 – Leonardo da Vinci's Top Ten Inventions

Now let's explore another search example, but this time we'll apply an iterative search approach as was presented in Chapter 2 to produce the results we're looking for. The search objective for this example is to identify Leonardo da Vinci's top ten inventions.

With our search objective defined, we begin preparing our Search Planning for by identifying the keywords, formulating the search query, and adding the derived search query by translating any, and all, specifications to the planning form, as shown in Figure 3-3. Then, the derived search query is entered in the Google search box to produce a list of results containing the timeline of Leonardo da Vinci's inventions, as shown in Figure 3-4. Due to the large number of results, we make modifications to the search query by revising the Search Planning form, as shown in Figure 3-5. The revisions include removing the keywords, 'timeline' and 'Renaissance man' in hopes of reducing the number of results.

Leonardo da Vinci's Top Ten Inventions

1. Define the topic and objectives for the search you want to conduct.

    Identify Leonardo da Vinci's top ten inventions

2. List the primary requirements associated with your search. Include special conditions, considerations, time periods, geographical regions, languages, prices, and other parameters.

    Requirement 1:   *Leonardo da Vinci*

    Requirement 2:   *timeline, Renaissance man, inventor*

    Requirement 3:   *top ten, top 10, inventions*

    Requirement 4:   *English language, all content types (filetypes)*

3. List keywords, synonyms, terms and phrases for your search query.

Requirement 1	Requirement 2	Requirement 3	Requirement 4
Leonardo	*timeline*	*top ten*	*all languages*
Da Vinci	*Renaissance man*	*top 10*	*all content*
Inventor	*inventions*		

4. Prepare your search using keywords, synonyms, phrases, requirements, logical & comparison operators, special operators, punctuation symbols, etc.

    Leonardo da Vinci and timeline or renaissance man
    or inventor and top ten or top 10 or inventions and
    English language and all content

Figure 3-3. Search Planning Form for Leonardo da Vinci's Top Ten Inventions

Leonardo da Vinci's Top Ten Inventions

1. Define the topic and objectives for the search you want to conduct.

   Identify Leonardo da Vinci's top ten inventions

2. List the primary requirements associated with your search. Include special conditions, considerations, time periods, geographical regions, languages, prices, and other parameters.

   Requirement 1:   *Leonardo da Vinci*

   Requirement 2:   *timeline, Renaissance man, inventor*

   Requirement 3:   *top ten, top 10, inventions*

   Requirement 4:   *English language, all content types (filetypes)*

3. List keywords, synonyms, terms and phrases for your search query.

Requirement 1	Requirement 2	Requirement 3	Requirement 4
Leonardo	*timeline*	*top ten*	*all languages*
Da Vinci	*Renaissance man*	*top 10*	*all content*
Inventor	*inventions*		

4. Prepare your search using keywords, synonyms, phrases, requirements, logical & comparison operators, special operators, punctuation symbols, etc.

   ["Leonardo da Vinci" AND (timeline OR renaissance man OR inventor) AND (top ten OR top 10) AND inventions]

Figure 3-4. Search Planning Form for Leonardo da Vinci's Top Ten Inventions

Example: **Identifying Leonardo da Vinci's Top Ten Inventions.**

Search: **["Leonardo da Vinci" AND (timeline OR renaissance man OR inventor) AND (top ten OR top 10) AND inventions]**

Results: **About 5.2 million results in 0.41 seconds.**

(This search produces way too many results, so revising the Search Planning form in in order!)

"Leonardo da Vinci" AND (timeline OR renaissance man OR inventor) AND (to 🔍   Q

Web   Images   Videos   Shopping   News   More ▾   Search tools

About 5,200,000 results (0.41 seconds)

Top 10 Leonardo da Vinci Inventions | Stuff of Genius ✅
www.geniusstuff.com/blog/list/10-leonardo-da-vinci-inventions/ ▾
Jun 21, 2013 - **Top 10 Leonardo da Vinci Inventions**. BY Christopher .... it is
interesting about how such an complacated **man** could be so talented. Reply · Like.

Science and **inventions** of Leonardo da Vinci - Wikipedia ... ✅
en.wikipedia.org/.../Science_and_inventions_of_Leonardo_da... ▾ Wikipedia ▾
Leonardo da Vinci (1452–1519) was an Italian polymath, regarded as the epitome
of the "Renaissance Man", displaying skills in numerous diverse areas of study. ... 9
Leonardo's projects; **10** Models based on Leonardo's drawings; 11 See also .... and
includes a **great** deal about the visual effects of light on different natural ...

Leonardo da Vinci - Wikipedia, the free encyclopedia ✅
en.wikipedia.org/wiki/Leonardo_da_Vinci ▾ Wikipedia ▾
Style, High **Renaissance** ... Leonardo's drawing of the Vitruvian **Man** is also
regarded as a cultural icon, being ... **[10]** Leonardo had no surname in the modern
sense, "da Vinci" simply ... He discovered a cave and was both terrified that some
great monster might ..... Main article: Science and **inventions** of Leonardo da Vinci.

Images for **"Leonardo da Vinci" AND (timeline OR ...**
Report images

Leonardo da Vinci's Top Ten Inventions

1. Define the topic and objectives for the search you want to conduct.

   Identify Leonardo da Vinci's top ten inventions

2. List the primary requirements associated with your search. Include special conditions, considerations, time periods, geographical regions, languages, prices, and other parameters.

   Requirement 1:   *Leonardo da Vinci*

   Requirement 2:   *top ten, top 10*

   Requirement 3:   *inventor, inventions*

   Requirement 4:   *English language, all content types (filetypes)*

3. List keywords, synonyms, terms and phrases for your search query.

Requirement 1	Requirement 2	Requirement 3	Requirement 4
Leonardo	*top ten*	*inventor*	*all languages*
Da Vinci	*top 10*	*inventions*	*all content*

4. Prepare your search using keywords, synonyms, phrases, requirements, logical & comparison operators, special operators, punctuation symbols, etc.

   ["Leonardo da Vinci" AND (top ten OR top 10) AND (inventor OR invention)]

**Figure 3-5. Revised Search Planning Form for
Leonardo da Vinci's Top Ten Inventions**

Basic Search

Iterative Search

Example: **Identifying Leonardo da Vinci's Top Ten Inventions.**

Search: **["Leonardo da Vinci" AND (top ten OR top 10) AND (inventor OR invention)]**

Results: **About 240 thousand results in 0.45 seconds.**

(The revised search produces fewer results than the original!)

"Leonardo da Vinci" AND (top ten OR top 10) AND (inventor OR invention)

Web   Shopping   Videos   Images   News   More ▾   Search tools

About 240,000 results (0.45 seconds)

Top 10 Leonardo da Vinci Inventions | Stuff of Genius
www.geniusstuff.com/blog/list/10-leonardo-da-vinci-inventions/ ▾
Jun 21, 2013 - Top 10 Leonardo da Vinci Inventions. BY Christopher ... Tagged
countdowns, inventions, inventor, leonardo da vinci, renaissance. + View ...

Leonardo Da Vinci's 10 Best Ideas | LiveScience
www.livescience.com/11329-leonardo-da-vinci-10-ideas.html ▾ LiveScience ▾
Nov 23, 2005 - Da Vinci helped revolutionize science. And sometimes he just
dreamed up fanciful concepts. Always, he thought in ways no one else had.

Top 10 Leonardo da Vinci Inventions | Utkarsh Prateek Blog
utkarshprateekblog.wordpress.com/.../top-10-leonardo-da-vinci-inventio... ▾
by Utkarsh Prateek
Jun 27, 2013 - Leonardo da Vinci may well have been the greatest inventor in
history, yet he had very little effect on the technology of his time. Da Vinci drew ...

Science and inventions of Leonardo da Vinci - Wikipedia ...
en.wikipedia.org/.../Science_and_inventions_of_Leonardo_da... ▾ Wikipedia ▾
Leonardo da Vinci (1452–1519) was an Italian polymath, regarded as the epitome
... he was, during his lifetime, employed for his engineering and skill of invention. ...
9 Leonardo's projects; 10 Models based on Leonardo's drawings; 11 See also ....
and includes a great deal about the visual effects of light on different natural ...
Condensed biography - Approach to scientific ... - Leonardo's notes and journals

What Did Leonardo DA Vinci Invent? - Ask.com
www.ask.com › Q&A › Arts and Humanities › Art ▾
What Did Leonardo Da Vinci Invented the solar power, musical instrument, ... MIT -
http://web.mit.edu/invent/iow/davinci.html · Museum of Science, Boston - http://

Example: Blog Post - Top 10 Leonardo da Vinci Inventions.

Search: ["Leonardo da Vinci" AND (top ten OR top 10) AND (inventor OR invention)]

Results: Blog Post – Top 10 Leonardo da Vinci Inventions.

Top 10 Leonardo da Vinci Inventions

BY CHRISTOPHER LAMPTON / POSTED JUNE 21, 2013

f Like 26   Tweet 47   8+ Share 79   reddit this!   SHARE WITH YOUR FRIENDS

Da Vinci's designs were spectacularly ahead of his time. If they had actually been built, they might have revolutionized the history of technology. What were some of his most imaginative sketches?

>> **START THE COUNTDOWN**   « PREV | NEXT »

Image
Results

Iterative
Search

Example: **Top 10 Leonardo da Vinci Inventions Images.**

Search: **["Leonardo da Vinci" AND (top ten OR top 10)**
AND (inventor OR invention)]

Results: **Images – Top 10 Leonardo da Vinci Inventions.**

  "Leonardo da Vinci" AND (top ten OR top 10) AND (inventor OR invention)   Q

Web   Shopping   Videos   Images   News   More ▾   Search tools

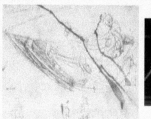

Search for Books with Google's Book Search

Bookworms rejoice! Whether you're searching for the latest bestseller, a scholarly textbook, non-copyrighted text in books, a cookbook of culinary favorites, a comic book with your favorite action hero, or an upcoming book title, Google's Book Search website is for you. The Google Book Search website is a popular destination for the avid reader.

Google's Book Search for Bookworms and Researchers

Google's Book Search is available for the bookworm in all of us, see Table 3-3.

Google Book Search Website	Description
Google Book Search – http://books.Google.com/	Google's Book Search website gives users the ability to search for bestsellers, textbooks, cookbooks, comics, upcoming book titles, non-copyrighted text in books, and much more.

Table 3-3. Google's Book Search Website

Example: **Searching books with Google Books User Interface.**

Search: **[books.Google.com]**

Results: **Google books (books.Google.com) website.**

Researching a topic?

Search the latest index of the world's books. Find millions of great books you can preview or read for free.

Search Books

Browse books and magazines »

New! Shop for Books on Google Play

Browse the world's largest eBookstore and start reading today on the web, tablet, phone, or ereader.

Google play

Go to Google Play Now »

My library

About Google Books - Privacy Policy - Terms of Service - Blog - Information for Publishers - Report an issue - Help - Sitemap - Google Home

©2012 Google

Example: **Searching astronomy books on books.Google.com**

Search: **[astronomy]**

Results: **Displays a list of astronomy topics in a drop-down list.**

Example: **Searching astronomy books on books.Google.com**

Search: **[astronomy]**

Results: **Over 12.8 million results in 0.54 seconds.**

Google astronomy

Web   News   Images   Videos   **Books**   More ▾   Search tools

About 12,800,000 results (0.54 seconds)

Bad **Astronomy**: Misconceptions and Misuses Revealed, from ...
books.google.com/books?isbn=047142207X
Philip C. Plait - 2002 - Preview - More editions
'The Truth Is Out There' and it's in this book. I loved it!" --Mike Mullane,
Space Shuttle astronaut and author of Do Your Ears Pop in Space?
Advance praise for Philip Plait?s Bad Astronomy "Bad Astronomy is just
plain good!

Fundamental **Astronomy**
books.google.com/books?isbn=3540341447
Hannu Karttunen, Pekka Kröger, Heikki Oja - 2007 - Preview - More
editions
While emphasizing both the astronomical concepts and the underlying
physical principles, the text provides a sound basis for more profound
studies in the astronomical sciences.

The Physical Universe: An Introduction to **Astronomy**
books.google.com/books?isbn=0935702059
Frank H. Shu - 1982 - Preview - More editions
This is a truly astonishing book, invaluable for anyone with an interest in
astronomy. Physics Bulletin Just the thing for a first year university
science course. Nature This is a beautiful book in both concept and
execution.

Astronomy: A Self-Teaching Guide
books.google.com/books?isbn=0470481463
Dinah L. Moché - 2009 - Preview - More editions
Discover the wonders of the night sky with this bestselling Astronomy
Guide For a generation, Astronomy: A Self-Teaching Guide has

Search for Scholarly Literature with Google Scholar

Google Scholar provides easy access to a broad range of scholarly literature. With the standard Google Scholar user interface, users have a powerful tool to search across disciplines for scholarly texts, books, abstracts, citations, authors, articles, theses, and court opinions from online resources such as universities, database repositories, academic publishers, professional organizations and societies, and scholarly websites.

Google Scholar enables users to conduct comprehensive worldwide literature searches quickly and easily. Full-text scholarly publications, related works, articles, citations, authors, and other resources are found and ranked. Once ranked, details about where and when the literature was published, who it was written by, as well as how recently and how often it is cited in scholarly journals and sources are provided. Google Scholar provides two methods of accessing electronic and print content:

- **Library Search** – provides links to textbooks, monographs and other bibliographic material in library book catalogues. Participation in a national or regional union catalog such as, OCLC's Open WorldCat, is required.

- **Library Links** – provides links to full-text journals, conference articles and electronic resources in libraries. An OpenURL-compatible link resolver such as, LinkSource from EBSCO, is required.

Google Scholar Literature Search for Researchers

Google Scholar provides a wonderful tool for authors, librarians, and researchers everywhere, see Table 3-4.

Google Book Search Website	Description
Google Scholar Search – http://Scholar.Google.com/	Google Scholar provides authors, librarians, and researchers with the capability to conduct scholarly literature searches across a broad range of disciplines in an easy-to-use user interface.

Table 3-4. Google Scholar User Interface

Example: **Searching with the Google Scholar User Interface.**

Search: **[Scholar.Google.com]**

Results: **Google Scholar (Scholar.Google.com) website.**

📂My library   ✏ My Citations   ✉ Alerts   📊Metrics   ⚙Settings

◉ Articles (✓ include patents)   ○ Case law

Stand on the shoulders of giants

Example: **Searching astronomy literature on Scholar.Google.com.**

Search: **[astronomy]**

Results: **About 2.39 million results in 0.05 seconds.**

Google   astronomy

Scholar   About 2,390,000 results (0.05 sec)

Articles

Case law

My library

[CITATION] Stochastic problems in physics and **astronomy**
S Chandrasekhar - Reviews of modern physics, 1943 - APS
Page 1. Page 2. Page 3. Page 4. Page 5. Page 6. Page 7. Page 8. Page 9. Page 10. Page 11.
Page 12. Page 13. Page 14. Page 15. Page 16. Page 17. Page 18. Page 19. Page 20. Page
21. Page 22. Page 23. Page 24. Page 25. Page 26. Page 27. Page 28. Page 29. Page 30. Page ...
Cited by 7779   Related articles   All 7 versions   Cite   Save   More

Any time
Since 2014
Since 2013
Since 2010
Custom range...

The effects of atmospheric turbulence in optical **astronomy**
F Roddier - In: Progress in optics. Volume 19. Amsterdam, ..., 1981 - adsabs.harvard.edu
Abstract Atmospheric turbulence is examined in terms of its effects on optical **astronomy**. The
statistical properties of atmospheric turbulence are explored, considering structure,
temperature and humidity fluctuations, and the dependence of the contribution of ...
Cited by 1137   Related articles   All 3 versions   Cite   Save   More

Sort by relevance
Sort by date

✓ include patents
✓ include citations

✉ Create alert

[BOOK] Adaptive optics in **astronomy**   [PDF] from tiera.ru
F Roddier - 1999 - books.google.com
Adaptive optics is a powerful new technique used to sharpen telescope images blurred by
the Earth's atmosphere. This authoritative book is the first dedicated to the use of adaptive
optics in **astronomy**. Mainly developed for defence applications, the technique of adaptive ...
Cited by 584   Related articles   All 11 versions   Cite   Save   More

[HTML] The X-ray **astronomy** satellite ASCA   [HTML] from harvard.edu
Y Tanaka, H Inoue, SS Holt - Publications of the Astronomical ..., 1994 - adsabs.harvard.edu
L3 Fig. 1. The X-ray **astronomy** satellite ASCA. Fig. 3. The focal plane detectors mounted on the
base plate of the spacecraft. For SIS and GIS, see text. STT is the star tracker. A part of the truss
structure of the extensible optical bench is also seen. Y. TANAKA et al. (see Vol. ...
Cited by 1059   Related articles   All 5 versions   Cite   Save

[BOOK] The decade of discovery in **astronomy** and astrophysics   [HTML] from google.com
National Research Council (US). Astronomy... - 1991 - books.google.com
The National Research Council commissioned the **Astronomy** and Astrophysics Survey
Committee, a group of 15 astronomers and astrophysicists, to survey their field and to
recommend new ground-and space-based programs for the coming decade. Support was ...

Basic
Search

Google
Scholar
Alert

Example: **Creating a Literature Alert with Google Scholar.**
Search: **[astronomy]**
Results: **Creating a Google Scholar Alert with results sent**
to your email address.

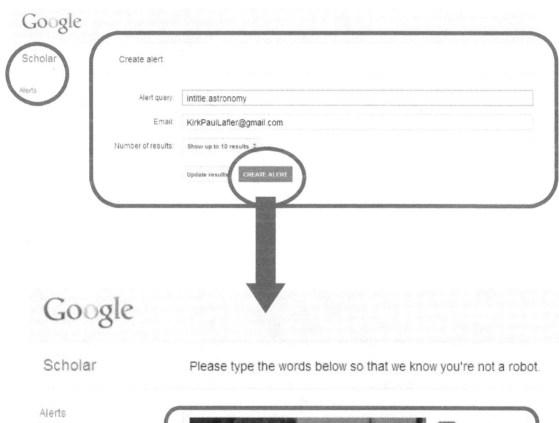

Google

Scholar

Alerts

Create alert

Alert query: intitle:astronomy

Email: KirkPaulLafler@gmail.com

Number of results: Show up to 10 results

Update results CREATE ALERT

Google

Scholar

Alerts

Please type the words below so that we know you're not a robot.

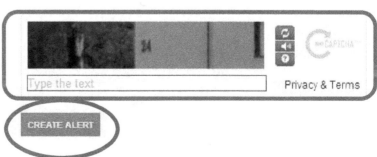

24

reCAPTCHA

Type the text

Privacy & Terms

CREATE ALERT

~ Chapter 4 ~

Using Punctuation Symbols for Better Searching

Google Punctuation Symbols

Google provides a number of punctuation symbols for a more enhanced search experience. A list of the punctuation symbols are illustrated in Table 4-1, below.

Punctuation Symbol	Description
~	Although the tilde punctuation symbol is no longer supported in Google searches, it used to display a list of synonyms in the search results.
@	The @ punctuation symbol produces results about social tags such as, [@google], [@sasnerd] and [@shippahoy].
#	The # punctuation symbol searches for trending hashtag topics such as, [#ilovegoogle] or [#googleisgreat].
$	The $ punctuation symbol searches for topics with a specified price such as, ["google book" < $50]. For example, [AS $400] produces different results than [AS 400].
%	The % punctuation symbol provides a percentage of some specified value. For example, [75% of 100] produce a result of 75.
&	The & punctuation symbol searches for strongly connected ideas or phrases such as, [peanut butter&jelly].
-	The – punctuation symbol is used for hyphenated words enabling keywords to be connected together such as, [word-of-mouth] or [2-day classes]. **Note:** A blank space should precede a – (minus sign) to avoid confusing it with a hyphenated word.
_	The _ (underscore) punctuation symbol permits word linking or word connections such as, [hash_tag] or [cost_effective].
+	The + (plus sign) allows popular terms and/or things containing a "+" to be searched such as, [C++], [google+], [google+ business], or [AB+].
Comparison Operators	The various comparison operators; = (equal), < (less than), > (greater than), <= (less than or equal), >= (greater than or equal); can be specified as punctuation symbols such as, ["google book" < $50].

Table 4-1. Google Punctuation Symbols

Example: **Producing results for the @google social tag.**

Search: **[@google]**

Results: **937,000 results in 0.61 seconds.**

Google | @google

Web News Images Shopping Maps More ▾ Search tools

About 937,000 results (0.61 seconds)

A Googler (google) on Twitter
https://twitter.com/google ▾
A Googler Verified account. @google. News and updates from Google. Mountain
View, CA · google.com. Tweets. Following. Followers. 4,845 400 8.26M ...

Google Nice!   View photo Hide photo
@google Nice! Wednesday, October   Text follow google to 40404 in the
21, 2009 | By Ev...   United States

More results from twitter.com »

Talks at Google - YouTube
www.youtube.com/user/AtGoogleTalks ▾
YouTube & @Google Talks present Anderson Cooper. by Talks at Google; 340,706
views. CC. Thumbnail Watch Later 1:07:42 ...

@Google Talks - YouTube
www.youtube.com/playlist?list=PLE84D6A52E72E45F2 ▾ YouTube ▾
39:48. Thumbnail Watch Later · @Google Talks presents Martha Stewart in
Conversation with Marissa Mayer · Talks at Google. 49:46. Thumbnail Watch Later

AtGoogleTalks - Wikipedia, the free encyclopedia
en.wikipedia.org/wiki/AtGoogleTalks ▾ Wikipedia ▾
AtGoogleTalks (or @Google Talks or Talks@Google) is a series of presentations by
invited speakers sponsored by Google given at various Google offices ...

Official Google Blog: 1000 @Google Talks videos now on YouT...
googleblog.blogspot.com/.../1000-google-talks-videos-now-on-youtube.... ▾
Mar 21, 2011 - Last week, the @Google Talks team uploaded its 1000th video to
YouTube. If you're not familiar with this series, we host talks by authors and ...

Spirit Junkie @Google | Gabrielle Bernstein, Inc.
gabbyb.tv/blogging/google ▾
"Gorras Lana Obey Baratas" hi there, ilog on to your reading named "Spirit Junkie
@Google | Gabrielle Bernstein, Inc." daily. Your humoristic style is awesome ...

Google

3,882,916 followers on Google+

Follow

Google is an American multinational
corporation specializing in Internet-related
services and products. These include search,
cloud computing, software, and online
advertising technologies. Most of its profits
are derived from AdWords. Wikipedia

Founded: September 4, 1998, Menlo Park, CA

Headquarters: Mountain View, CA

CEO: Larry Page

Founders: Larry Page, Sergey Brin

Recent posts

April 15 is approaching fast and if that date means
nothing to you, we'd recommend setting a reminder
for yourself ASAP. In the Google Search app, just say,
"OK ... 3 hours ago

People also search for

  Aol.

Skype   Yahoo!   AOL   Apple Inc.   Amazon....

Feedback

Example: **Searching trending hash tag topics.**
Search: **[#ilovegoogle]**
Results: **73 results in 0.33 seconds.**

Google   #ilovegoogle   🎤   🔍

Web   Maps   Images   Shopping   Videos   More ▾   Search tools

About 73 results (0.33 seconds)

#ilovegoogle - Photos tagged **ilovegoogle** on Instagram - 5th v...
instavillage.com/ilovegoogle/ ▾
My first ever end of year gift as a teacher from @onebiscuitplease_13 & I just love
it. Just Google it... does get said in my Writing For. ladymelbourne 1 day ago.

Instagram photos for tag **#ilovegoogle** | Statigram
statigr.am/tag/ilovegoogle ▾
Browse all Instagram photos tagged with #ilovegoogle. View likes and comments.

#ilovegoogle - Photos tagged **ilovegoogle** on Instagram - 5th v...
pagespeed.5thvillage.com/ilovegoogle/ ▾
#thursty #thirsty #thirstyHOES #trying to #fakeittomakeit #movearound #
fuckYODRAMA #igotme #getyours #iLOVEgoogle #hahahahha #youmadornaww.

Hashtag - **#ilovegoogle**
www.totally.me/hashtagtrends/allaboutoomf/hashtag/ilovegoogle ▾
Mar 29, 2014 - #Google #ilovegoogle #tiny Just got a Chromebook. Only Web based
services is weird, but you know what? I really like the little thing! #Google ...

Hashtag - **#Ilovegoogle** - Totally.me
www.totally.me/MarinaCastro/marina/hashtag/ilovegoogle ▾
Dec 1, 2013 - Google celebrating our national day with us! #UAE #ilovegoogle
#google http://t.co/xJCNmFytZ3 Google celebrating our national day with us!

Definition of Hashtag **#ilovegoogle** - Hashtags.org
www.hashtags.org/definition/ilovegoogle/ ▾
Jan 22, 2014 - Definition of Hashtag #ilovegoogle: This is a hash tag for people to
post stuff, comment, video, audio on Google.

Ilovegoogle | Tag Feed | Instagrin
instagr.in/t/ilovegoogle ▾
Sep 10, 2013 - ilovegoogle tag feed. Instagrin is a web version of Instagram that
allows anyone to browse through user, tag, and location feeds. Sign in with ...

Example: **Searching books under $50.**

Search: **["google book" < $50]**

Results: **Over 1 million results in 0.65 seconds.**

Google   "google book" < $50   🎤   🔍

Web   Shopping   News   Images   Videos   More ▾   Search tools

About 1,010,000 results (0.65 seconds)

Fifty Things Under **$50** Bucks To Promote Your Book | Author ...
www.amarketingexpert.com/fifty-things-under-50-bucks-to-promote-yo... ▾
Fifty Things Under $50 Bucks To Promote Your Book. by: Penny. Enter Your Mail
Address ... Add your book to Google Book Search. 29.) Research some authors ...

Fifty Things Under **$50** Bucks To Promote Your Book | Author ...
www.amarketingexpert.com/fifty-things-under-50-bucks-to-promote-yo... ▾
28) Add your book to Google Book Search. 29) Research some authors with similar
subjects and then offer to exchange links with them. 30) Is your book good ...

Fifty Things Under **$50** Bucks To Promote Your Book - Huffingto...
www.huffingtonpost.com/.../fifty-things-under-50-b... ▾ The Huffington Post ▾
Nov 16, 2009 - Fifty Things Under $50 Bucks To Promote Your Book. What's Your
Reaction: ... 28) Add your book to Google Book Search. 29) Research some ...

Other Services - WingSpan Press - Book Publishing | Self-Publi...
www.wingspanpress.com/other_services.php ▾
Google Book Search submission -- $50. When people search for books on Google
your book will be available for review, with links to major retailers for ...

The **Google Book** Settlement: a survival aid for UK authors
www.gillianspraggs.com/gbs/GBS_survival_aid.html ▾
The Amended Google Book Settlement agreement, if accepted by the court, ... $200
(£120) per book; $50 (£30) per 'Entire Insert'; $25 (£15) per 'Partial Insert'.

The **$50** e-book-capable tablet: When will the Harvard-hosted D...
 librarycity.org/?p=1583 ▾
by David Rothman - in 251 Google+ circles
Jun 15, 2011 - The $50 e-book-capable tablet: When will the Harvard-
hosted DPLA and ... E-books catching on in K-12—plus the rejection of the
Google Book ...

Example: **Searching books between $1 and $20.**

Search: **["google book" $1 . . $20]**

Results: **Over 500 thousand results in 0.50 seconds.**

Google   "google book" $1 .. $20   🎤   🔍

Web   Shopping   News   Images   Videos   More ▾   Search tools

About 543,000 results (0.50 seconds)

How authors can add books to Google Books - Books Help
https://support.google.com/books/answer/43782?hl=en ▾ Google ▾
The best way to get your books included is to speak with your publisher and
encourage them to join the Google Books Partner Program. You can direct them to ...

Book Sales in Maryland
www.booksalefinder.com/MD.html ▾
Hours: 10:00 AM to 5 PM; $20 Early Admission at 8:00 AM; Numbers handed out ...
Prices from $1 to $20; special selections higher: Separate checkout lines at ...

Google co-founders took $1 salary in 2013 - Rediff Realtime News
realtime.rediff.com/news/...took.../654391fbb939af19?... ▾ Rediff.com ▾
Google co-founders took $1 salary in 2013 ... Facebook takes leaf out of Google's
book with Oculus buy. Times of In.., 4 ... Google chairman paid nearly $20m.

Pre-reading - Oncology Massage Training
www.oncologymassagetraining.com.au/index.php?content=39 ▾
To purchase these, check out Google Book Depository first as they have cheaper
prices ... Amazon.com and www.fishpond.com.au and retails for about US$20.

Pay for More Gmail Storage - Google Operating System - Blogger
googlesystem.blogspot.com/2007/08/pay-for-more-gmail-storage.html ▾
Aug 9, 2007 - So for $20 a year, you'll get 6 GB that can be used to store photos in ...
the price for the 6 GB option was $1, but Google quickly changed it to $20.) .... New
Context Menus in Google Docs - The Quality of Google Book Search ...

Premium Fixed-layout eBook Package- Little Pond Publishing, Inc.
www.littlepondpublishing.com/.../premium-publishing-package-fixed-la... ▾
Book cover copywriting (includes one draft; $20 fee per revision applies). • Your own
... Your eBook's metadata and content listed in the Google Book Search

Example: **Producing a percentage of a specified value.**

Search: **[70% of 9.99]**

Results: **Over 3.8 million results in 0.42 seconds.**

Google | 70% of 9.99

Web   Shopping   News   Images   Videos   More ▾   Search tools

About 3,850,000 results (0.42 seconds)

70% of 9.99 =

6.993

Rad		x!	(	)	%	AC
Inv	sin	ln	7	8	9	÷
π	cos	log	4	5	6	×
e	tan	√	1	2	3	-
Ans	EXP	x'	0	.	=	+

More info

$9.99 regular price? **70**% off on 9/13 - PlaystationTrophies.org
www.playstationtrophies.org/.../123607-9-99-regular-price-70-off-9-13-... ▾
Sep 7, 2011 - Is this game's regular price now **$9.99**? I saw a thread dated last
march talking about **$9.99** being a short-lived sale price. As of right now, ...

How much is **9.99** plus 30%? - Yahoo Answers
https://answers.yahoo.com/question/index?qid... ▾
Mar 30, 2012 - I need to know what would be the price of a shirt if it was **9.99** take an
... You need to know what **70**% of the price is (100% = **9.99**, 30% off ...

List Price Requirements - Amazon Kindle Direct Publishing: Get ...
https://kdp.amazon.com/help?topicId=A301WJ6XCJ8KW0 ▾ Amazon.com ▾
Greater than 3 megabytes and less than 10 megabytes, $ 1.99, $ 200.00. • 10
megabytes or greater, $ 2.99, $ 200.00. **70**% Royalty Option, $ 2.99, $ **9.99** ...

Example: **Searching popular terms like "C++" in a search query.**

Search: **["C++ tips"]**

Results: **23.3 thousand results in 0.43 seconds.**

Google   "C++ tips"   🎤 🔍

Web   Videos   Images   Shopping   News   More ▾   Search tools
_____

About 23,300 results (0.43 seconds)

C/C++ Programming Tips and Tricks - Cprogramming.com
www.cprogramming.com/tips/ ▾
30+ items - Source Code Snippets   C and C++ **Tips**   Finding a Job.

Tip   Author
Make pointer and reference arguments const   Akshay
Using _strtime and _strdate to get the time   Ali Jafar
The power of scanf() - Make pointer and reference ... - Tip - What is a friend function?

The Top 20 **C++ Tips** of All Time - DevX
www.devx.com/cplus/Article/16328 ▾
Feb 15, 2001 - The Top 20 C++ **Tips** of All Time. What makes these tips special is
that the information they provide usually cannot be found in C++ books or ...

Tips and Tricks - C++ Articles - Cplusplus.com
www.cplusplus.com/articles/tips/ ▾
20+ items - Search: Articles; Tips and Tricks. Articles : Tips and Tricks ...
PowerBall Lottery Simulator Revamped   fimas.   Mar 14, 2014
Turbo C++ 3.1 Code Example For A List Box   analyzoh.   Mar 5, 2014

[PDF] The C++ Programming Language **C++ Tips** and Traps ...
www.cs.wustl.edu/.../C++-tips-n-traps... ▾ Washington University in St. Louis ▾
C++ **Tips** and Traps. Outline. Tips for C Programmers. C++ Traps and Pitfalls. E
ciency and Performance. 1. Tips for C Programmers. Use const instead of de ne ...

C++ Tip-of-the-Day
www.cpptips.com/cpptips.html ▾
Welcome to the C++ Tip-of-the-Day. This is a compilation of information gathered
from various sources below. The purpose of this free service is to keep ...

Microsoft Visual **C++ Tips** and Tricks - High Programmer
www.highprogrammer.com › Alan De Smet › Windows Development ▾
Microsoft Visual C++ **Tips** and Tricks. by Alan De Smet. If you're stuck using Microsoft
Visual C++, these tips may help make the experience more pleasant.

_____

Example: Searching blood types in a search query.
Search: ["AB- type"]
Results: 646 thousand results in 0.52 seconds.

Google   "AB- type"   🎤 🔍

Web   Images   Shopping   Videos   News   More ▾   Search tools

About 646,000 results (0.52 seconds)

Blood type - Wikipedia, the free encyclopedia
en.wikipedia.org/wiki/Blood_type ▾ Wikipedia ▾
A blood type (also called a blood group) is a classification of blood based on the
presence or absence of inherited antigenic substances on the surface of red ...
Blood type distribution by country - ABO - Blood group systems - Rh

See results about

ABO blood group system
The ABO blood group system is the most important
blood type system in human blood transfusion. The ...

Feedback

Images for **"AB- type"**   Report images

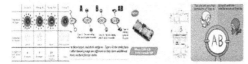

More images for **"AB- type"**

How To Target Type AB- - Donate Blood - One Blood
www.oneblood.org/target-your-type/ab-negative.stml ▾
AB- is the rarest of all the blood types with only 1% of the population sharing this
special power. Donors who are AB- are the universal platelet and plasma donor ...

People with AB Blood Type More Likely to Develop Clots ...
healthland.time.com/.../whats-in-a-blood-type-could-be-your-risk-o... ▾ Time ▾
Feb 4, 2013 - Not all individuals with **AB type** blood will develop clots, but the blood
type may be a relatively easy way to identify those who may be at higher ...

Donor Blood Type Information | NW Cryobank
https://www.nwcryobank.com/donor-blood-type-information/ ▾
Example 1. MOM-AB, **type** AB ≈-, A, B. DAD-B, **type** BO ≈, B, AB, child type AB, BB,
child type B, O, AO, child type A, BO, child type B ...

Cat Blood Group - UC Davis Veterinary Genetics Laboratory
https://www.vgl.ucdavis.edu/.../abblood.p... ▾ University of California, Davis ▾
A third rare type "AB" is also known. Cats with the rare **"AB" type** do not have anti-A

Example: **Using compound keywords in a search query.**

Search: **[launch-ready land-based AND (missiles OR rockets)]**

Results: **Over 1 million results in 0.63 seconds.**

Google launch-ready land-based AND (missiles OR rockets) 🔍 🔍

Web   Images   Shopping   News   Videos   More ▾   Search tools

About 1,050,000 results (0.63 seconds)

News for **launch-ready land-based AND (missiles ...**

U.S. to cut deployed nuclear **missiles** to 400
Press Herald - 2 hours ago
... number of deployed, **launch-ready** intercontinental ballistic
missiles ... of 450 **land-based** nuclear **missiles** but remove 50
from their launch ...

US will cut Air Force nuke missile force by 50
KMPH Fox 26 - 6 hours ago

More news for **launch-ready land-based AND (missiles OR rockets)**

To comply with treaty, US will cut Air Force and Navy ... - Fox News
www.foxnews.com/.../to-comply-with-treaty-us-will-c... ▾ Fox News Channel ▾
7 hours ago - The Obama administration says the number of **launch-ready** Air Force
land-based nuclear **missiles** will shrink to 400 — the lowest total since ...

US to cut Air Force nuclear arsenal by 50 **missiles** - 41 NBC News
www.41nbc.com/...**missiles**/.../jh6IN5xSpkWomCWdkdkj6... ▾ WMGT-TV ▾
5 hours ago - The Obama administration on Tuesday said the number of **launch-**
ready Air Force **land-based** nuclear **missiles** will shrink to 400 — the lowest ...

For nuclear security beyond Seoul, eradicate **land-based** 'doom...
www.csmonitor.com/.../For-nuclear-securi... ▾ The Christian Science Monitor ▾
Mar 27, 2012 - America's 450 **launch-ready land-based** nuclear-armed ballistic
missiles are the opposite of a deterrent to attack. In fact, their very deployment ...

Nuclear triad - Wikipedia, the free encyclopedia
en.wikipedia.org/wiki/Nuclear_triad ▾ Wikipedia ▾
They possess nuclear forces consisting of **land-based missiles**, ballistic or ..... and
launch ready deployment for the US and former USSR by the SALT II treaty.

~ Chapter 5 ~

Exploring Specialized Operators

"Powerful" Specialized Google Operators

Google provides a number of specialized operators to help with your search queries by finding information about a specific book, population number, investment fund, movies, public stock, unemployment rate, weather, or website; identifying and displaying information that Google has collected about backlinks (or incoming links) for a specific website; and display maps about a specific country, state, city, or location, as shown in Table 5-1.

Operator	Description	Example
area code <or> AREA CODE	Displays the geographical location for any three-digit area code or the three-digit area code for a specific city.	[AREA CODE 619] <or> [AREA CODE 310] <or> [AREA CODE san diego]
Book <or> BOOK	Searches and displays book-related information about the keyword entered.	[BOOK google]
define <or> DEFINE	Displays a definition for a specific word or phrase.	[DEFINE quasar] <or> [DEFINE analytics]
info <or> INFO	Displays information that Google has collected for a website.	[INFO www.google.com]
link <or> LINK	Displays backlinks (or incoming links) for a specific website or web page that is received from another website.	[LINK www.google.com]
location <or> LOCATION	Displays content only for the geographic location that is specified.	[LOCATION "San Diego"] < or > [LOCATION 92122]
map <or> MAP	Displays a map of a specific country, state, city or location.	[San Diego map]
movie <or> MOVIE	Searches and displays where a movie is currently playing and a description of all movies currently playing in a specific location.	[MOVIE bourne] <or> [MOVIE 91978] <or> [MOVIE spring valley]

Table 5-1. Specialized Google Operators

Operator	Description	Example
population <or> POPULATION	Displays the population of a U.S. state or county.	[POPULATION San Diego]
site <or> SITE	Displays the number of indexed pages for a specific website.	[SITE www.google.com]
site <or> SOURCE	Displays the specific news source for the selected content.	["2012 election" SOURCE wsj]
stock <or> STOCK	Displays the market data for a specific company's stock or fund.	[STOCK goog]
time <or> TIME	Displays the current time in a city.	[TIME Honolulu]
unemployment rate <or> UNEMPLOYMENT RATE	Display unemployment rate trends of a U.S. state, county or zipcode.	[UNEMPLOYMENT RATE San Diego] <or> [UNEMPLOYMENT RATE 91978]
weather <or> WEATHER	Display the weather conditions, temperature, humidity, wind, and forecast for many cities or zipcodes.	[WEATHER San Diego]

Table 5-1. Specialized Google Operators (continued)

Basic Search

Specialized Operators Example

Example: **Using the DEFINE operator for definitions to words.**

Search: **[DEFINE oceanography]**

Results: **1.2 million results in 0.49 seconds.**

 DEFINE oceanography

Web   Images   News   Shopping   Maps   More ▾   Search tools

About 1,270,000 results (0.49 seconds)

o·cea·nog·ra·phy
/ˌōSHəˈnägrəfē/ ◀)

noun

1. the branch of science that deals with the physical and biological properties and phenomena of the sea.

Oceanography - Definition and More from the Free Merriam ...
www.merriam-webster.com/dictionary/oceanography ▾ Merriam-Webster ▾
a science that deals with the oceans and includes the delimitation of their extent and depth, the physics and chemistry of their waters, marine biology, and the ...

Oceanography | **Define Oceanography** at Dictionary.com
dictionary.reference.com/browse/oceanography ▾
Oceanography definition, the branch of physical geography dealing with the ocean.
See more.

oceanography - definition of **oceanography** by the Free ...
www.thefreedictionary.com/oceanography ▾ TheFreeDictionary.com ▾
o·cean·og·ra·phy n. The exploration and scientific study of the ocean and its phenomena. Also called oceanology. o'cean·og'ra·pher n. o'cean·o·graph'ic ...

Oceanography - Wikipedia, the free encyclopedia
en.wikipedia.org/wiki/Oceanography ▾ Wikipedia ▾
Oceanography (compound of the Greek words ὠκεανός meaning "ocean" and γράφω meaning "write"), also known as oceanology and marine science, is the ...
Physical oceanography - Argo - Chemical oceanography - Mooring

---

Basic Search

Specialized Operators Example

Example: **Searching content located in a specific geographic area.**

Search: **[LOCATION "La Jolla California"]**

Results: **26 million results in 0.84 seconds.**

Google   location "la jolla california"   🎤   🔍

Web   Maps   Shopping   Images   News   More ▾   Search tools

About 26,000,000 results (0.84 seconds)

La Jolla - Wikipedia, the free encyclopedia
en.wikipedia.org/wiki/La_Jolla ▾ Wikipedia ▾
The University of California, San Diego (UCSD) is located in La Jolla, as are the
Salk Institute, Scripps … San Diego Historical Landmarks in La Jolla, California …

La Jolla - Home - Official site of La Jolla, California
www.lajollabythesea.com/ ▾ La Jolla ▾
The Official site of La Jolla, California with information on local hotels, dining,
shopping, services, beaches and events for visitors and residents in La Jolla, CA.
Visitor Information - Calendar - Dining - Beach Guide

La Jolla - Maps & Directions - Official site of La Jolla, California
www.lajollabythesea.com › Visitor Resources ▸ La Jolla ▾
Maps & Directions. La Jolla is located 15 miles north of downtown San Diego and
approximately two hours driving south from Los Angeles.

Bank of America   Ⓐ 8613 Villa La Jolla Dr
locators.bankofamerica.com   La Jolla, CA
2 Google reviews   (858) 552-4055

Sol Yoga Studios   Ⓑ 8657 Villa La Jolla Dr
www.solyogastudios.com   #121
4.6 ★★★★★ 9 Google reviews   La Jolla, CA
                               (858) 452-9842

FedEx Office Print & Ship Center Ⓒ 8849 Villa La Jolla Dr
local.fedex.com   La Jolla, CA
2.3 ★★★☆☆ 17 Google reviews   (858) 457-3775

La Jolla Sports Club   Ⓓ 7825 Fay Ave
www.lajollasportsclub.com   La Jolla, CA
4.8 ★★★★★ 5 Google reviews · Google+ page (858) 456-2595

Torrey Pines Golf Course   Ⓔ 11480 Torrey pines
www.sandiego.gov   park Rd
4.1 ★★★★☆ 249 Google reviews · Google+ page San Diego, CA

Map for **location "la jolla california"**

Ads ⓘ

La Jolla California
www.tripadvisor.com/La_Jolla ▾
Find Deals & Read Real Reviews.
La Jolla deals on TripAdvisor!

La Jolla California
www.wow.com/La+Jolla+California ▾
Search for La Jolla California
Look Up Quick Results Now!

Where Is La Jolla California
www.webcrawler.com/ ▾
Search multiple engines for
where is la jolla california

Map La Jolla CA
www.izito.com/Map+La+Jolla+CA ▾
Find Map La Jolla CA
In 6 Search Engines at Once.

Panerai Boutique
www.cjcharles.com/Panerai ▾
Panerai Boutique La Jolla
Panerai Luminor Radiomir & Service

Example: Searching content located in a specific country.
Search: [POPULATION canada]
Results: 348 million results in 0.66 seconds.

Web   Maps   Images   News   Videos   More ▾   Search tools

About 348,000,000 results (0.66 seconds)

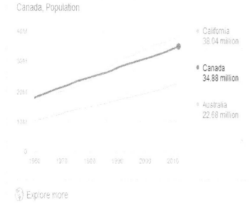

Canada

Country

Canada is a country in North America consisting of 10 provinces and 3 territories. Located in the northern part of the continent, it extends from the Atlantic to the Pacific and northward into the Arctic Ocean. Wikipedia

Related statistics

Gross domestic product	1.821 trillion USD (2012)
Population growth rate	1.1% annual change (2012)
Life expectancy	80.93 years (2011)

Population elsewhere

United States of America	313.9 million (2012)
China	1.351 billion (2012)
Russia	143.5 million (2012)

Sources include: World Bank, United States Census Bureau

Population of **Canada** - Wikipedia, the free encyclopedia
en.wikipedia.org/wiki/Population_of_Canada ▾ Wikipedia ▾
The historical growth of Canada's population is complex and has been influenced by several factors, such as indigenous populations, expansion of territory, and ...
Historical population overview - Components of population growth

List of **Canadian** provinces and territories by **population** ...
en.wikipedia.org/.../List_of_Canadian_provinces_and_territori... ▾ Wikipedia ▾
This is a list of Canadian provinces and territories by population based on Statistics Canada's 2011 census. Statistics Canada's most recent population ...

Canada - Wikipedia, the free encyclopedia
en.wikipedia.org/wiki/Canada ▾ Wikipedia ▾

Example: **Searching a specific website for content.**
Search: **["Networking Advice" SITE www.LinkedIn.com]**
Results: **79.3 thousand results in 0.48 seconds.**

Google   "Networking Advice" SITE www.LinkedIn.com

Web   Images   News   Shopping   Videos   More ▾   Search tools

About 79,300 results (0.48 seconds)

Networking Advice from a Recruiter | **LinkedIn**
www.linkedin.com/.../20140325010327-5002379-**networking**-... ▾ LinkedIn ▾
Mar 25, 2014 - I have always had a passion for helping job seekers and those trying
to be smarter about their career decisions. This is for you. Fair warning, it ...

Networking Rules for Job-seekers: the Good, the ... - **LinkedIn**
www.**linkedin.com**/.../20130916190035-15454-**networking**-rul... ▾ LinkedIn ▾
Sep 16, 2013 - Solutions to Challenges I Quality I Manufacturing I Engineering I
Operations I Supply Chain. Hey Lou, Thanks for the sound **networking advice**.

Networking Advice 9
www.calmoaa.org/index.php?option...**networking-advice-9**... ▾
Jul 26, 2013 - Site Admin. ... <http://www.linkedin.com/e/-a13g74-hjftn3iw-
3n/ava/259698697/1800872/eml-anet_dig-b_nd-pst_ttle-cn/?hs=false&tok= ...

Networking Advice 10
www.calmoaa.org/index.php?option...**networking-advice**... ▾
Jan 31, 2014 - Site Admin. ... <http://www.linkedin.com/e/-a13g74-hqy6tgcf-
12/vai/1800872/ ... 5 essential elements missing from your **LinkedIn** profile

Networking Advice 6
calmoaa.org/index.php?option=com...**networking-advice-6**... ▾
Mar 22, 2013 - Site Admin. ... Veterans: Unfortunately, It's Your Problem
<http://www.linkedin.com/e/-a13g74-hefn0qpl-
1m/vai/164686/221276015/member/eml ...

Networking Advice 8
www.calmoaa.org/index.php?option...**networking-advice-8**... ▾

Example: **Searching a specific source for content.**
Search: **["2012 Election" SOURCE wsj]**
Results: **3.6 million results in 0.63 seconds.**

Google   "2012 election" SOURCE wsj   🔍

Web   Shopping   Images   Videos   Maps   More ▾   Search tools

About 3,660,000 results (0.63 seconds)

2012 Election Polls - Projects Wsj - Wall Street Journal
projects.wsj.com/campaign2012/polls ▾ The Wall Street Journal ▾
Collection of the latest 2012 Election polls for the presidency. ... follow wsj election
coverage: ... 7, 2012 | Source: Real Clear Politics. Subscribe. Portfolio.

Politics and Election News - WSJ.com - Wsj.com
online.wsj.com/.../news-politics-campaign.html ▾ The Wall Street Journal ▾
WSJ complete coverage of the 2012 US presidential election and races for Senate,
House and Governor seats. News, polls, debates, primaries and results.

2012 Election Delegate Tracker - Presidential Race
projects.wsj.com/campaign2012/delegates ▾ The Wall Street Journal ▾
WSJ Europe; WSJ Americas. en Espa?ol · em Portugu?s · WSJ Radio · WSJ Wine
... Source: Associated Press. WSJ Web Slice. CONTENT. LINKS TO ACTUAL ...

What County-by-County Results Tell Us About the Election ...
online.wsj.com/.../SB10001424127887323894470... ▾ The Wall Street Journal ▾
The most detailed results from the 2012 election show the voting patterns for each
county in the country. ... 1 of 12 [http://s.wsj.net/public/resources/images ... Sources:
Associated Press (results), CoreLogic (housing), U.S. Bureau of Economic ...

2012 General Election Editorial Endorsements by Major ...
www.presidency.ucsb.edu/.../201... ▾ University of California, Santa Barbara ▾
100+ items - 2012 Election Documents. · 2008 Election Documents.

The Wall Street Journal   2,118,315   Generally does not endorse candidates.
USA Today   1,817,446   Does not endorse candidates.

RealClearPolitics - Latest Election Polls
www.realclearpolitics.com/epolls/latest_polls/elections/ ▾ RealClearPolitics ▾
National and state polls on candidates, campaigns and political issues, collected
from a variety of sources.

Other - President Obama Job Approval - Real Clear Politics
www.realclearpolitics.com/.../president_obama_job_app... ▾ RealClearPolitics ▾
The Dissing of the President - Bret Stephens, Wall Street Journal. - Obama's

---

Basic Search

Specialized Operators Example

Example: **Searching a stock symbol for financial information.**

Search: **[STOCK goog]**

Results: **Almost 7.9 million results in 0.60 seconds.**

Google STOCK goog

Web   News   Shopping   Videos   Maps   More ▾   Search tools

About 7,890,000 results (0.60 seconds)

Google
NASDAQ: GOOG - Apr 10 7:53 PM ET

540.95 -23.19 (-4.11%)
After Hours: 541.50 +0.55 (0.10%)

Open	565.00
High	565.00
Low	539.90
Volume	4,027,743
Avg Vol	2,255,000
Mkt Cap	380.81B

1d   5d   1m   6m   1y   5y   max

Google Finance - Yahoo Finance - MSN Money   Disclaimer

News for **STOCK goog**

After-Hours **Stock** News: **Google** Inc. (NASDAQ: GOOG ...
International Business Times - by Jessica Menton - 3 days ago
After the closing bell, shares of Google Inc., Expedia Inc. and Gigamon Inc. were among Monday's biggest **stock** movers.

Stock Market News for April 10, 2014
Zacks.com - 12 hours ago

More news for **STOCK goog**

GOOG: Summary for **Google** Inc.- Yahoo! Finance
finance.yahoo.com/q?s=GOOG ▾ Yahoo! Finance ▾
View the basic GOOG stock chart on Yahoo! Finance. Change the date range, chart type and compare Google Inc. against other companies.
GOOG Interactive Chart - Options - Historical Prices - Message Boards

Basic Search

Specialized Operators Example

Example: Searching for movies with a map of their locations.

Search: [MOVIE san diego MAP san diego]

Results: Movie listings with a map of San Diego.

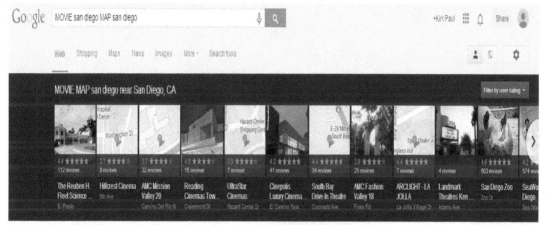

Movie Theatres in **San Diego**, California | MapQuest
www.mapquest.com/maps?...Movie%20Theatres...San%20Die... ▾ MapQuest ▾
Find Movie Theatres in **San Diego**, California provided by MapQuest. Find Movie
Theatres locations in your local area - maps, directions, and phone numbers.

San Diego Movie Listings | **San Diego** Showtimes, theaters ...
www.tributemovies.com › california ▾
Movie Theaters in **San Diego**, california. Click on a number to locate your theater on
the map below. 1 AMC Fashion Valley 18; 2 AMC Mission Valley 20; 3 AMC ...

San Diego Movie Theaters - Yellowpages.com
www.yellowpages.com › San Diego, CA › Yellowpages.com ▾
Results 1 - 30 of 31 - 31 listings of Movie Theaters in San Diego on YP.com. Find
reviews ... Address, ZIP Code, or Neighborhood: My current location. Search.

san diego crew gigs classifieds - craigslist
sandiego.craigslist.org › CL › san diego › gigs ▾ Craigslist Inc. ▾
Apr 10 Arri Kits, Kino Flo Kits and more (San Diego) pic map. Apr 10 video Editor
(SD) ... Apr 7 Camera Shooter wanted unique 48 hour film project pic map.

Entertainment Arts **Movie** Theaters in **San Diego**, CA on ...
https://local.yahoo.com/CA/San+Diego/.../Movie+Theaters ▾ Yahoo! Local ▾
Results 1 - 10 of 450 - Entertainment Arts Movie Theaters in San Diego, CA on ...

1   AMC Theatres Fashion Valley 18   (888) 262-4386   7037 Friars Rd
6   Landmark Theaters San Diego   (619) 819-0236   3965 5th Ave

Map for **MOVIE san diego MAP san diego**

~ Chapter 6 ~

General, Subject, Public and Private Database Searches

Database Searches

Google's search reach is nothing less than amazing. From general to subject to public to private databases, Google's ability to search for database archives of information empowers the researcher in all of us.

Google's search methods provide access to incredible quantities of content located anywhere on the web. But, not all content is available using a Google search. Often times, bibliographic content such as books, articles, journals, magazines, conference proceedings, papers, and other sources are only available for searching using online databases. These online sources of information fall into the following categories: general, subject, public and private databases.

General databases include broad coverage of newspaper, magazine and journal articles on a number of multidisciplinary topics. Unlike general databases, subject databases offer discipline-based, narrowly focused, research-related articles and publications of a scholarly nature. Public and private databases offer a combination of features generally found in both general and subject databases.

A common feature found in general, subject, public and private databases is the availability of integrated, built-in, user interfaces to simplify and streamline the search process. Typically, basic database searches support a single search box, while more advanced searches supports multiple search boxes.

Searching for Database Content

Here's some advice for conducting effective database searches:

1. Develop a list of words and synonyms related to your search;
2. Search the database thesaurus for terms associated with your topic;
3. Databases only search for the words you entered, and nothing else;
4. Use Boolean operators, (AND, OR, or NOT), to combine or link two or more words (or synonyms) in your search.

General Databases

- Scholarly articles, publications and materials;
- Military and religious libraries, archives and references;
- News, headlines and world current events.

General Database Types

General databases are online tools that are available for free or for a small fee. Anyone with a web browser can access their content including the full-text versions of scholarly magazines, academic journals, and newspaper articles. Examples of general databases include LexisNexis® Academic, Academic OneFile, and Academic Search Premier. A partial list of popular general databases for research purposes is shown in Table 6-1.

General Databases	Description
LexisNexis® Academic – http://www.lexisnexis.com/hottopics/ln academic/?	Provides a variety of authoritative sources including the full text of more than 350 newspapers from around the world, more than 300 magazines and journals, more than 600 newsletters, the Associated Press and Business Wire services, comprehensive business and financial news services, U.S. Supreme Court decisions, and much more.
Genealogy Public Databases	The top ten U.S. genealogy databases are: www.Ancestry.com, www.familysearch.org, www.rootsweb.com, www.worldvitalrecords.com, www.genealogybank.com, www.familytreeconnection.com, www.archives.gov/genealogy/.

Table 6-1. General Databases

General Databases	Description
National Institute of Health (NIH) - http://report.nih.gov/searchable_public_databases/	NIH supports biomedical research to enhance health, lengthen life, and reduce the burdens of illness and disability. It provides a number of searchable public databases including: RePORTER, NIDB Resources, NCBI Literature Databases, PubMed Central, PubMed (Medline), Research.gov, Community of Science, Science.gov, World Wide Science, and Clinical Trials.gov.
Medford Public Schools http://www.medfordpublicschools.org/schools/medford-high-school/student-services/library-media-center/free-public-databases/	Several free databases are available: Occupational Outlook Handbook (http://www.bls.gov/ooh/), CIA World Factbook (https://www.cia.gov/library/publications/the-world-factbook/index.html), American Civil War Resources (http://spec.lib.vt.edu/civwar/), United States Holocaust Memorial Museum (http://www.ushmm.org/), Medline Plus (http://www.nlm.nih.gov/medlineplus/), Windows to the Universe (http://www.windows2universe.org/windows.html).

Table 6-1. General Databases (continued)

Example: **Searching for general databases.**
Search: **[general databases]**
Results: **Over 144 million results in 0.39 seconds.**

Google | general databases 🎤 🔍

Web   News   Images   Videos   Shopping   More ▾   Search tools

About 144,000,000 results (0.39 seconds)

Types of **Databases** - University of Illinois
www.library.illinois.edu/.../d... ▾ University of Illinois at Urbana-Champaign ▾
Being aware of what this scope is can be helpful in selecting a **database** to begin
your information search. **General** interest **databases** include information from ...

General Databases at the LIU Post Library ◔
www2.liu.edu/cwis/cwp/.../database/general.htm ▾ Long Island University ▾
General OneFile (InfoTrac/Gale Group) Remote access available NOVEL **Database**
Full text available: Formerly InfoTrac OneFile, a one-stop source for news ...

General vs. subject specific resources - Ask Us/Get Help
gethelp.library.upenn.edu/PORT/.../generalvsspecific.ht... ▾ Van Pelt Library ▾
Jul 18, 2013 - Library databases vs. www. *. Subject-specific vs. **general databases**.
*. Types of searches. *. Keyword searching. *. Subject searching.

General Databases - NCSU Libraries - North Carolina State ...
www.lib.ncsu.edu/databases/general-data... ▾ North Carolina State University ▾
A description for this result is not available because of this site's robots.txt – learn
more .

Palomar College Library - Online **Databases** - **General** ◔
www.palomar.edu/library/onlinedatabases/databases.htm ▾ Palomar College ▾
Online Research Databases. (Off-campus ... **General Databases**. Academic Search
Premier (EBSCO), Open Database Display Database Description. This is a ...

General Databases - Databases - LibGuides at St. Joseph's ... ◔
sjcny.libguides.com/content.php?pid=146754&sid=1262749 ▾
General Databases. The following are databases that cover most subject areas.

Basic Search

Database Search Example

Example: **Searching for general research databases.**
Search: **[general research databases]**
Results: **Over 716 million results in 0.36 seconds.**

Google | general research databases 🔍 🔍

Web   Images   News   Shopping   Videos   More ▾   Search tools

About 716,000,000 results (0.36 seconds)

General Research Databases
https://go.dmacc.edu/.../resgenerald... ▾ Des Moines Area Community College ▾
General Research Databases. MasterFile Premier From EBSCOhost - a database
covering virtually all topics of general interest, the majority available in full text.

Top 10 Online **Databases** for **General Research** | Everest ...
fmuonline.wordpress.com/.../top-10-online-databases-for-general-researc... ▾
Jan 24, 2007 - Here is a list of the top 10 online research databases for general
research: Academic Search Elite (EBSCO) ABI/INFORM Complete...

Full-text **General Research Databases** - Weekend Masters ...
guides.lib.purdue.edu › LibGuides ▾ Purdue University ▾
Jan 10, 2014 - These databases have full-text articles linked from most of the
citations. The subject coverage is broad and interdisciplinary and the databases ...

The Clinical Practice **Research** Datalink (CPRD)
epi.grants.cancer.gov/pharm/...db/cprd.html ▾ National Cancer Institute ▾
Dec 20, 2013 - The CPRD is the world's largest database of anonymized, ... cancer
in the General Practice Research Database compared with national cancer ...

Palomar College Library - Online **Databases** - **General**
www.palomar.edu/library/onlinedatabases/databases.htm ▾ Palomar College ▾
Online Research Databases. (Off-campus ... General Databases. Academic Search
Premier (EBSCO), Open Database Display Database Description. This is a ...

Multidisciplinary/**General Research Databases**
libguides.tncc.edu/content.php?pid=223979&sid=1878317
To search databases, you can use the complete A-Z annotated list of databases,

Example: **Searching for general reference databases.**
Search: **[general reference databases]**
Results: **Over 490 million results in 0.37 seconds.**

Google | general reference databases   🎤   🔍 |

Web   Images   Shopping   News   Videos   More ▾   Search tools

About 490,000,000 results (0.37 seconds)

General and **Reference** - Articles & **Databases** - LibGuides ...
uri.libguides.com/ref ▾
Sep 26, 2013 - Databases: General and Reference Print Page. Search Text Search
... This guide provides a list of all of URI's general databases. The lists are ...

NMSU Library **General Reference Databases** ✅
lib.nmsu.edu/resources/gperlist.shtml ▾ New Mexico State University ▾
Nov 8, 2013 - General Reference Databases. Unless otherwise indicated, remote
access to these databases is available only to NMSU faculty, students, and ...

General Reference Databases — Mercer University Libraries ✅
libraries.mercer.edu › ... › Databases › Subjects ▾ Mercer University ▾
Dec 11, 2013 - Academic Search Complete (EBSCO) — Provides abstracts and
indexing for over 3,800, as well as full text for over 3,200 scholarly journals ...

General Reference Databases - University of Massachusetts ... ✅
libweb.uml.edu › ... › Databases Home ▾ University of Massachusetts Lowell ▾
General Reference Databases. UML Home ... Databases | eBooks | Research
Guide. Search multiple databases using Ebsco's Discovery Service. Keyword Title

General Reference Databases | Semans Library | UNC ... ✅
library.uncsa.edu/home/e-resources/subjects/General%20Reference ▾
10+ items - General Reference Databases. Click to view all database ...
Biography Reference Center.   Full-text of biographical reference books
Encyclopedia Britannica.   The encycloepdia online

SCU University Library - **General Databases** & **Reference** ... ✅
www.scu.edu › ... › Databases by Subject ▾ Santa Clara University ▾

Example: **Searching for the LexisNexis® Academic database.**

Search: **[lexis nexis academic]**

Results: **Over 1.8 million results in 0.36 seconds.**

Google   lexis nexis academic   🎤   🔍

Web   Shopping   News   Images   Maps   More ▾   Search tools

About 1,860,000 results (0.36 seconds)

Lexis-Nexis Academic Universe ✅
web.**lexis-nexis**.com/universe ▾
A description for this result is not available because of this site's robots.txt – learn more .

Academic | Legal Research for Students | **LexisNexis**® ✅
academic.lexisnexis.com/ ▾ LexisNexis ▾
With more than 15,000 business, legal and news sources, **LexisNexis Academic** offers one of the most robust and thorough research tools available to college ...
Academic & Library Solutions - Academic and Library - LexisNexis Academic

Lexis Nexis Academic - Contact Us ✅
academic.lexisnexis.eu/ ▾
A description for this result is not available because of this site's robots.txt – learn more .

LexisNexis Academic | The Library ✅
libraries.ucsd.edu › Resources ▾ University of California, San Diego ▾
LexisNexis Academic. URL. http://uclibs.org/PID/20081. Description. Thousands of full-text sources including newspapers, wires, transcripts, newsletters, ...

LexisNexisAcademic - YouTube ✅
www.youtube.com/user/LexisNexisAcademic ▾
View Tutorials on a variety of LexisNexis products. ... **LexisNexis Academic**: Finding Landmark US Cases. 1,570 views; 4 months ago. Thumbnail Watch Later

Databases - **LexisNexis Academic** ✅
www.lib.utexas.edu › ... › Databases ▾ University of Texas at Austin ▾

Example: **Searching the LexisNexis® Academic database.**
Search: **[lexis nexis academic]**
Results: **LexisNexis® Academic Search database.**

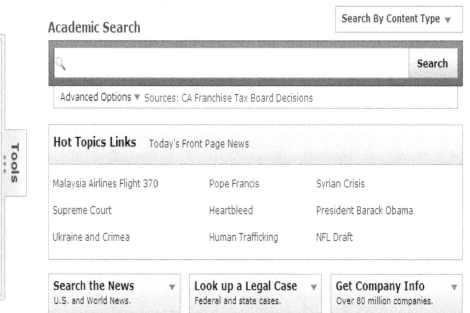

Subject, Public and Private Databases

Subject, Public and Private databases are generally available for free or are fee-based and can be accessed by anyone using a web browser. The subject, public and private databases in Table 6-2 include a few sources for research purposes.

Types of Subject, Public and Private Databases

- Business, economics, labor statistics and entrepreneurship;
- Government databases and datasets;
- Finance, investment and real estate;
- Health, medical and pharmaceutical;
- Education, teaching, library science and professional development;
- Trends, popular culture, entertainment and sports;
- Patents, copyrights and trademarks;
- Mathematics, computer science, statistics and engineering;
- Biological and chemical sciences, physics and astronomy;
- Blogs, bulletin boards, groups and social networking;
- Shopping, travel and merchandising;
- Political science, biographical, legal, philosophy, psychology and sociology;
- History, communication, archaeology, paleontology and earth science;
- Religion, literature, languages, art and music;
- Maps, images and graphics.

Subject, Public and Private Databases	Description
Enigma - http://enigma.io/	Enigma accesses more than 100,000 public data sources published by governments, companies and organizations. According to Enigma, the types of data sources include state and federal records, SEC filings, lists of frozen assets, environmental violations, patents, liens, healthcare providers, medicare reimbursements, U.S. census, national labor market activity, daily weather data, aviation incidents, real estate foreclosures, oil and gas production by well, and much more.

Table 6-2. Subject, Public and Private Databases

Subject, Public and Private Databases	Description
National Institute of Health (NIH) - http://report.nih.gov/searchable_public_databases/	NIH supports biomedical research to enhance health, lengthen life, and reduce the burdens of illness and disability. It provides a number of searchable public databases including: RePORTER, NIDB Resources, NCBI Literature Databases, PubMed Central, PubMed (Medline), Research.gov, Community of Science, Science.gov, World Wide Science, and Clinical Trials.gov.
Genealogy Public Databases	The top ten U.S. genealogy databases for tracing your family tree: www.Ancestry.com, www.familysearch.org, www.usgenweb.com, www.rootsweb.com, www.footnote.com, www.worldvitalrecords.com, www.genealogybank.com, www.godfrey.org, www.archives.gov/genealogy/, www.familytreeconnection.com.
Bureau of Labor Statistics - http://data.bls.gov/cgi-bin/surveymost?bls	The Bureau of Labor Statistics (BLS), an independent statistical agency, of the U.S. Department of Labor and is the principal Federal agency responsible for measuring labor market activity, working conditions, and price changes in the economy. BLS collects, analyzes, and disseminates essential economic information to support public and private research by providing products and services that are objective, timely, accurate, and relevant.
Medford Public Schools http://www.medfordpublicschools.org/schools/medford-high-school/student-services/library-media-center/free-public-databases/	Several free databases are available: Occupational Outlook Handbook (http://www.bls.gov/ooh/), CIA World Factbook (https://www.cia.gov/library/publications/the-world-factbook/index.html), American Civil War Resources (http://spec.lib.vt.edu/civwar/), United States Holocaust Memorial Museum (http://www.ushmm.org/), World War I Document Archive (http://www.gwpda.org/), Medline Plus (http://www.nlm.nih.gov/medlineplus/), Google Earth (http://www.google.com/earth/), Windows to the Universe (http://www.windows2universe.org/windows.html),

Table 6-2. Subject, Public and Private Databases (continued)

Subject, Public and Private Databases	Description
University of Nebraska-Lincoln http://unl.libguides.com/content.php?pid=284621&sid=2342340	The University of Nebraska-Lincoln offers several public databases for community users including: NebraskAccess (http://nebraskaccess.ne.gov/), Government Documents (http://libraries.unl.edu/govdocs), Agricultural Literature (http://agricola.nal.usda.gov/), PubMed (http://www.ncbi.nlm.nih.gov/pubmed/), WolrdCat (http://www.worldcat.org/), ArchiveGrid (http://beta.worldcat.org/archivegrid/), Image and Multimedia Collections (http://contentdm.unl.edu/).
The Washington Post Public Databases http://www.washingtonpost.com/wp-srv/metro/data/datapost.html	The Washington Post Public Databases include: All About Schools (http://www.washingtonpost.com/wp-srv/metro/data/washington-area-schools-2011-2012.html), Malls in America (http://www.washingtonpost.com/wp-srv/business/charts/malls.html), Census and Demographics (http://factfinder2.census.gov/faces/nav/jsf/pages/index.xhtml), High School Rankings (http://apps.washingtonpost.com/local/highschoolchallenge/).
United States Coast Guard Library Academy Subject Databases http://libguides.uscga.edu/subjectdatabase	The United States Coast Guard Library Academy of Subject Databases include: General Multi-Subject Databases; Business & Economics; Engineering & Technology; Health Sciences, Psychology & Medicine; Military, Intelligence & Homeland Security; Political Science, Law & Government; Science; Social Science, Education & Humanities; News & Current Events; Language Resources; and Reference Resources.
EhIS (EBSCOhost Integrated Search) http://andersonuniversity.libguides.com/content.php?pid=261781&sid=2161147	EhIS (EBSCOhost Integrated Search) enables searches across multiple databases at one time including access to full-text search of articles, eBooks, journals, and scholarly and peer-reviewed publications.

Table 6-2. Subject, Public and Private Databases (continued)

Example: **Searching for subject databases.**

Search: **[subject databases]**

Results: **Over 97.3 million results in 0.34 seconds.**

Google | subject databases | 🔍 | Q

Web   Images   Videos   News   Shopping   More ▾   Search tools

About 97,300,000 results (0.34 seconds)

Types of **Databases** - University of Illinois
www.library.illinois.edu/.../d... ▾ University of Illinois at Urbana-Champaign ▾
Databases can be organized by the scope of the information they contain. ... General
interest **databases** include information from several different **subject** areas ...

Library Tutorial: Choosing a database | **Subject databases** ✅
ica.library.oregonstate.edu/.../401--Library-Tuto... ▾ Oregon State University ▾
Tutorials & Guides This unit introduces you to the **subject databases**. **Subject**
databases are a good place to find scholarly materials written for people in the ...

Subject Specific **Databases** - Auraria Library ✅
library.auraria.edu/tutorials/**subject**-specific-**databases**
🔲 When you need articles in a specific discipline, try using **subject databases**.
This tutorial covers the basics for finding and selecting one.

Subject Databases - Articles and Databases - LibGuides at ... ✅
hbl.gcc.libguides.com/content.php?pid=272611 ▾
To search **databases**, you can use the complete A-Z annotated list of **databases**,
search **databases** by **subject**, or locate the course-specific libguide.
Religion - Education - Communication - History

General vs. **subject** specific resources - Ask Us/Get Help ✅
gethelp.library.upenn.edu/PORT/.../generalvsspecific.ht... ▾ Van Pelt Library ▾
Jul 18, 2013 - Library **databases** vs. www. *. **Subject**-specific vs. general **databases**.
*. Types of searches. *. Keyword searching. *. **Subject** searching.

All Subjects - **Databases** To Get You Started - **Subject** and ... ✅
libguides.lib.uci.edu/**databases** ▾ University of California, Irvine ▾

Example: **Searching for the Enigma database.**

Search: **[enigma database]**

Results: **Over 2.7 million results in 0.36 seconds.**

Google | enigma database | 🎤 | 🔍

Web   Videos   Images   Shopping   News   More ▾   Search tools

About 2,760,000 results (0.36 seconds)

Enigma
enigma.io/ ▾
Search and analyze billions of public records published by governments, companies
and organizations. **Enigma** empowers the world to discover public data and ...
About - Sign Up - Press - Sign In

Evidence-based Network for the Interpretation of Germline ...
enigmaconsortium.org/ ▾
Jul 16, 2013 - ENIGMA is a consortium of investigators focused on determining the
involvement ... Use of the ENIGMA website and **database**, and associated ...
Eligibility - Contacts - Meetings - Publications

Enigma brings the deep, dark world of public data to light ...
venturebeat.com/.../enigma-brings-the-deep-dark-world-of-... ▾ VentureBeat ▾
May 1, 2013 - **Enigma** launched out of beta today to shed light on this hidden world.
... Engima's **database** contains billions of public records across more than ...

Enigma.io (Beta) - **Databases** - Baker Library | Bloomberg ...
www.library.hbs.edu › ... › Browse AZ Listing ▾ Harvard Business School ▾
Enigma.io (Beta). Go to **Database**. Description: Extracts and summarizes data from
disparate public **databases** that can be searched and browsed within one ...

Enigma Interactive - **Database** Developers | **Database** ...
www.enigmainteractive.com/software/database-development/ ▾
Our expertise with **database** development covers the entire development cycle of
designing, developing and deploying robust and reliable **database** solutions.

Example: **Searching the Enigma.io database.**
Search: **[enigma database]**
Results: **Enigma database.**

Example: **Searching for Bureau of Labor Statistics (BLS) database.**

Search: **[bls database]**

Results: **Over 2.5 million results in 0.58 seconds.**

Google | bls database | 🎤 🔍

Web   Images   News   Videos   Shopping   More ▾   Search tools

About 2,540,000 results (0.58 seconds)

Databases & Tables - Bureau of Labor Statistics
www.**bls**.gov/data/ ▾ U.S. Bureau of Labor Statistics ▾
Database Name, Special Notice, Top Picks, One Screen, Multi- Screen, Tables, Text
Files. Prices - Consumer. All Urban Consumers (Current Series) (Consumer ...

CPI Databases
Average Price Data - Inflation
Calculator - Urban Consumers

Consumer Price Index-All ...
Consumer Price Index-All Urban
Consumers -- Seasonal (Screen ...

Average Price Data
Consumer Price Index-Average
Price Data (Select from list ...

Occupational Employment ...
Occupational Employment
Statistics. (For more information ...

CES Databases
(Current Employment Statistics -
CES), Special Notice, Top ...

Database Administrators
Database administrators (DBAs)
use specialized software to ...

More results from bls.gov »

Occupational Employment Statistics Home Page
www.**bls**.gov/oes/ ▾ U.S. Bureau of Labor Statistics ▾
OES **Databases**. Databases. **Database** Name, Multi- ... Text Files links you to the
BLS FTP server, where you can view text files of the data behind the ...

U.S. Bureau of Labor Statistics
www.**bls**.gov/ ▾ U.S. Bureau of Labor Statistics ▾
The **Bureau of Labor Statistics** is the principal fact-finding agency for the Federal ...
Discontinued **Databases** · FAQs · Special Notices · More Sources of Data.

Example: **Searching the Bureau of Labor Statistics (BLS) database.**

Search: **[bls database]**

Results: **Bureau of Labor Statistics (BLS) database.**

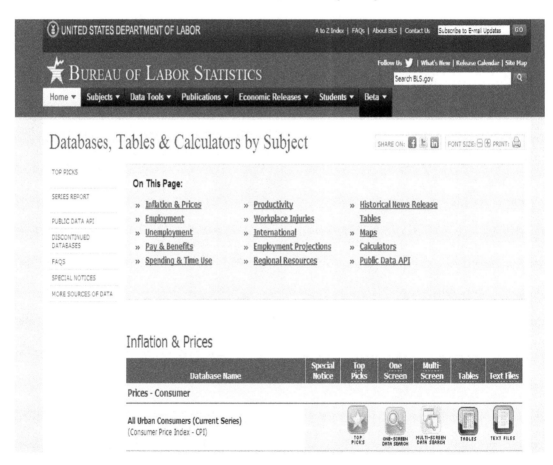

~ Chapter 7 ~

Too Few Results, Too Many Results, or Results Not Relevant – Tips, Tricks and Shortcuts for Getting the Results You Want

Too Few Results

Are you the victim of receiving too few results from your search? Or, have you taken the necessary time to prepare, what you believed was, a comprehensive search plan including the identification of one or more keywords that express your idea or search topic, only to find the search results to be too few? You are not alone. Many searchers express some level of disappointment and disbelief when they find their search produces an unexpected and disappointing too few results. If you are the beneficiary of this all too familiar complaint, then don't despair. The following tips, tricks and shortcuts may help you out of your predicament.

1. Check your search query for typos. As you would expect, a typo in any of your keywords can directly impact the results of your search.

2. Check your search query against the search results. Identify any additional keywords and/or phrases that can be used to expand the search results to a greater and more desired number.

3. Check your search query to determine if searching against a general or specific subject database(s) would yield a greater number of search results.

4. Check your search query to see if any of your keywords should be removed. The use of too many keywords, referred to as keyword overloading your search query, forces the search engine to look for all the keywords resulting in the delivery of too few results.

5. Check your search query for contradictory keywords. For example, "hubble space telescope microscope", produces too few results because of the contradictory nature of the terms "telescope" and "microscope".

6. Check your search query for the existence of implied "ANDed" operators between multiple keywords. Multiple keywords with blank spaces between them are automatically interpreted by the Google search engine as if an implied "AND" operator is specified. For example, the keywords, "hubble space telescope", is interpreted by the Google search engine as "hubble" AND "space" AND "telescope", meaning that all keywords must appear in the search results.

7. Check your search query to see if quoted phrases can be modified to include an "OR" operator between any of the keywords. An "OR" operator between multiple keywords tells the Google search engine to broaden the search horizon by allowing any of the keywords to appear in the search results.

8. Check your search query for the existence of quoted phrases. A quoted phrase forces the Google search engine to find content using the exact keywords in the order specified. For example, a search query containing the quoted phrase, "hubble space telescope", may be more restrictive (or return fewer search results) than if the quotes were removed.

> An "OR" operator between multiple keywords broadens the search horizon by allowing any of the keywords to appear in the search results.

Example: **Searching for health-related information.**

Search: **[how many calories in a big mac large fries coke apple pie filetype:pdf $1 .. $1.50]**

Results: **33 results in 0.65 seconds.**

Google   how many calories in a big mac large fries coke apple pie filetype:pdf $1 .. $1.5 🎤 🔍

Web   Shopping   Images   News   Videos   More ▾   Search tools

33 results (0.65 seconds)

[PDF] Menu - Off the Traxx
www.offthetraxx.com/wp-content/uploads/finalmenu13.pdf ▾
Have your Chicken done: Parmesan crusted, **Fried**, Blackened or Grilled .... **Big** Easy
Crawdaddy Pasta ... **large** salad or have a bowl of soup and a ... Not your mom's
apple pie, our ... Traxx we have just cut the **calories** in half. ... Diet Pepsi - Club **Soda**
- Bottle Water $1.99 ... Tap Water It's on Shawn, I know it's too **much**!
Missing: ~~mac~~

[PDF] Carry Out Menu - Bob Evans
bobevans.com/.../Bob_Evans_Carry_Out_Menu.p... ▾ Bob Evans Restaurants ▾
bacon or hickory-smoked ham, hash browns, home **fries** or grits** and choice of
specialty .... UNDER 450 **CALORIES** ... seasonal topping, or blueberry topping to your
hotcakes for **$1** ... **Big** Farm Hamburger Green leaf lettuce, red onion, deli pickles
and tomato Combo .... Farming is in our heritage, so a delicious **apple pie** is.
Missing: ~~mac~~

[PDF] Appetizers - Cowfish
https://www.thecowfish.com/The_Cowfish_menu.pdf ▾
Calamari tubes & tentacles, flash **fried** and served with a sweet chili calamari
sauce. 12 .... Half-pound turkey burger, Brie cheese, sweet cranberries, Fuji **apples**,
spicy ... Garlic & Herb Boursin Cheese. Black Truffle Cheese (**$1.50**). **$1** per. Protein:
.... **Large** 5. - Fiji Still or Perrier Sparkling. SOFT DRINKS - **Coke**, Sprite, Diet ...

[PDF] Our Menu - Shante
www.theshante.com/.../Shante%20Fall%20&%20Winter%202013%20&... ▾
bread for **$1.50** less. Sorry, no ½ ... Add **Chips** & veggies for an additional $1.00. ....
Big or Little ... MAC N' CHEESE. $3.75 **Apple** Sauce/Fruit Cup 85¢ ... Healthy Choice
CHICKEN BLT SALAD (402 **calories**) ... 7" Flatbread 12"Medium 14"**Large** ...
Chicken Pot **Pie** $6.10 ... pizza's & get 8 cookies AND a 2 Liter of **Soda**...

Example: **Expanding results by removing keywords.**

Search: **[how many calories in a big mac large fries coke apple pie filetype:pdf]**

Results: **7.2 thousand results in 0.40 seconds.**

(This search produces more results than the previous search!)

Google   how many calories in a big mac large fries coke apple pie filetype:pdf   🎤   🔍

Web   Shopping   Images   News   Videos   More ▾   Search tools

About 7,260 results (0.40 seconds)

[PDF] McDonald's USA **Nutrition** Facts for Popular Menu Items
nutrition.mcdonalds.com/getnutrition/nutritionfacts.pdf ▾ McDonald's ▾
We provide a **nutrition** analysis of our menu items to help you balance your
McDonald's meal with other foods you eat. Our goal is ... Vitamin A. Vitamin C.
Calcium. Iron. Burgers & Sandwiches. **Big Mac.** 7.6 oz ...... **Apple** Slices† ... 15.
Large French. **Fries.** 5.4 oz. (154 g)500 220. 25. 38. 3.5. 17. 0. 0. 0. 350. 15 ... Diet
Coke®.

[PDF] Heat Part I (Chapter 6) - Campbell
web.campbell.edu/.../CHEM%20113%20Chapter6.H... ▾ Campbell University ▾
Dietary **calories** (Cal or kcal) ... **Many** energy changes are `state ... **Big Mac.** 530.
250. 28. **Large Fries.** 450. 200. 22. SuperSize **Fries.** 540. 230. 26 ... A **Big Mac,**
Super-size **Fries,** Hot **Apple Pie** and a Diet. **Coke** (i.e.being **calorie** conscious).

[PDF] McDonald's **Calorie** Counter
www.dossmanntech.com/.../McDonald's%20calorie%20counter.pdf ▾
Have you heard of the **calorie** shifting diet? Quick prep ... **Big Mac.** 7.8 oz. 25 47 30
13.5. 560 MORE. Big N' Tasty. 8.2 oz. 24 41 23. 11. 470 MORE ... **Large** French **Fries.**
6 oz .... Baked **Apple Pie.** 2.7 oz ... Coca-Cola Classic (Medium). 21 fl oz ...

[PDF] **Nutrition** Facts - McDonald's
www1.mcdonalds.ca/NutritionCalculator/NutritionFa... ▾ McDonald's Canada ▾
Nutrition Facts. As of May ... Double **Big Mac®** sandwich. 268g 700 ..... **Apple** Slices
with Caramel Dip. 89g 100 ... French **Fries** - **Large** .... Diet **Coke®** - Medium.

[PDF] Chapter 7_Bio28
www.laney.edu/wp/asha.../files/.../Chapter-7_Bio28.pdf ▾ Laney College ▾
Calories in Vs Calories out ... Use these websites to figure out **how many** cal you

---

Example: **Expanding results by removing special operators.**

Search: **[how many calories in a big mac large fries coke apple pie]**

Results: **117 thousand results in 0.46 seconds.**

(This search produces even more results than the previous search!)

Google   how many calories in a big mac large fries coke apple pie   🎤   🔍

Web   Shopping   Images   News   Videos   More ▾   Search tools

About 117,000 results (0.46 seconds)

Full Menu Explorer :: McDonalds.com
www.mcdonalds.com/us/en/full_menu_explorer.html ▾ McDonald's ▾
My Meal Builder 0 items. **Big Mac**. Quarter Pounder with Cheese. Bacon Clubhouse
Burger. Bacon Habanero Ranch Quarter Pounder. Bacon & Cheese Quarter ...

[PDF] McDonald's USA **Nutrition** Facts for Popular Menu Items
nutrition.mcdonalds.com/getnutrition/nutritionfacts.pdf ▾ McDonald's ▾
We provide a **nutrition** analysis of our menu items to help you balance your
McDonald's meal with other foods you eat. Our goal is ... Vitamin A. Vitamin C.
Calcium. Iron. Burgers & Sandwiches. **Big Mac**. 7.6 oz ...... **Apple** Slices† ... 15.
Large French. **Fries**. 5.4 oz. (154 g)500 220. 25. 38. 3.5. 17. 0. 0. 0. 350. 15 ... Diet
Coke®.

HowStuffWorks "Fast-food Safety and **Nutrition**"
 science.howstuffworks.com/.../fast-food2.htm ▾ HowStuffWorks ▾
by Tracy Wilson - in 287 Google+ circles
A **Big Mac**, **large fries**, baked **apple pie** and large **Coke** ... can consume
almost as **many calories** and sodium and more fat than you should
consume in a day.

McDonald's **Calorie** Counter (CalorieLab)
calorielab.com/restaurants/mcdonalds/1 ▾
Calorie counts and complete **nutrition** facts for McDonald's from the CalorieLab
Nutrition Database. ... **Big Mac**, 7.8 oz, 25, 47, 30, 13.5, 560, MORE. Big N' Tasty, 8.2
oz, 24, 41, 23, 11 ... Menu Category: French **Fries** .... Baked **Apple Pie**, 2.7 oz, 2, 34,
11, 6, 250, MORE ... Diet **Coke (Large)**, 32 fl oz cup, 0, 0, 0, 0, 0, MORE.

McDonald's **Calorie** Chart

Too Many Results

In direct contrast to receiving too few results, (as discussed in the previous section), you may be the victim of receiving an unexpected and overwhelming number of results from your search. If this is the case, don't despair; simply consider the following tips, tricks and shortcuts to help you out of your all too common predicament and begin reducing the quantities of results to a more manageable size.

1. Check your search query against the results to determine if adding one or more relevant keywords can help to further narrow your search results.

2. Check your search query for the use of wildcards, specified with an asterisk "*". A wildcard enables the Google search engine to search a word that can end a multiple number of ways. As you would expect, a wildcard in your search query can directly increase the number of results you receive.

3. Check your search query for the occurrence of any "OR" operators between multiple keywords. When an "OR" operator is used between keywords, you are typically asking the Google search engine to broaden your search results. For example, the keywords, "hubble OR space OR telescope", produces an abundance of results that include content containing the word, "hubble", or "space", or "telescope". One way to reduce the results in the previous example would be to change the "ORs" in the search query to "ANDs", as follows, "hubble AND space AND telescope", to restrict the results so that all keywords would appear in the search results.

4. Check you search query against the produced results to see if there are any keywords that are producing "false" hits, or results that have nothing to do with your search. Consider using a minus sign, "-", before a word or phrase to negate (or eliminate) it from the search results.

5. Check your search results to determine if you can narrow or limit content by publication date, by file type (i.e., pdf, doc, xls, ppt, etc.), or some other content-reducing parameter.

6. Check your search results to determine if limiting the search to a specific subject database could limit content to a more desirable level.

7. Use Google **Search tools** to reduce results – this is an iterative approach, see example later in this chapter.

**Basic
Search**

**Too
Many
Results**

Example: **Asking Google for suggestions on healthy eating.**
Search: **[suggestions for healthy eating]**
Results: **42.5 million results in 0.53 seconds.**
(This search produces way too many results!)

Google   suggestions for healthy eating   🎤   🔍

Web   News   Images   Videos   Shopping   More ▾   Search tools

About 42,500,000 results (0.53 seconds)

Healthy Eating: Easy **Tips** for Planning a **Healthy Diet** ...
www.helpguide.org/life/healthy_eating_diet.htm ▾
Healthy eating is about eating smart. Transform your eating habits with these easy
tips.
Diet & Nutrition for Women - Diet & Weight Loss - Eating Well Help Guide
- Nutrition

Healthy Eating Tips - ChooseMyPlate.gov ☑
www.choosemyplate.gov/**healthy-eating-tips**.html ▾ MyPlate ▾
These **tips** and **ideas** are a starting point. You will find a wealth of **suggestions** here
that can help you get started toward a **healthy diet**. Choose a change that ...

10 **Tips** Nutrition Education Series - ChooseMyPlate.gov ☑
www.choosemyplate.gov › Printable Materials and Ordering ▾ MyPlate ▾
These **tips** and **ideas** are a starting point. You will find a wealth of **suggestions** here
that can help you get started toward a **healthy diet**. Choose a change that ...

ChooseMyPlate.gov ☑
www.choosemyplate.gov/ ▾ MyPlate ▾
As MyPlate Ambassadors, students can champion **healthy eating** at their schools.
ChooseMyPlate. ... Easy to follow **tips** for consumers and professionals alike.

Healthy Every Week: **Healthy Meals** and Recipes
www.foodnetwork.com › Healthy Eating ▾ Food Network ▾
Get **healthy** recipes, how-tos and **tips** from Food Network for every day of the week -
from **healthy**, easy weeknight dinners to weekend appetizer recipes and ...

Example: **Reducing the number of results by selecting past year.**

Search: **[suggestions for healthy eating]**

Results: **Select "Past year" from Search tools to reduce results.**

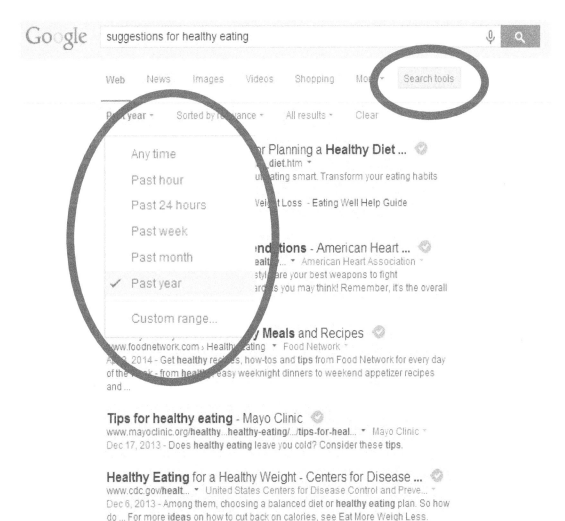

Example: **Reducing the number of results to past year.**

Search: **[suggestions for healthy eating]**

Results: **2.27 million results in 0.48 seconds.**

(This iterative approach produces fewer results!)

Google   suggestions for healthy eating   🎤   🔍

Wet   Videos   Shopping   More ▾   Search tools

About 2,270,000 results (0.48 seconds)

Healthy Eating: Easy **Tips** for Planning a **Healthy Diet** ...
www.helpguide.org/life/**healthy_eating_diet**.htm ▾
Feb 15, 2014 - **Healthy eating** is about eating smart. Transform your eating habits
with these easy **tips**.
Diet & Nutrition for Women - Diet & Weight Loss - Eating Well Help Guide
- Nutrition

Diet and Lifestyle **Recommendations** - American Heart ... ⊘
www.heart.org/.../GettingHealthy/.../Healthy... ▾ American Heart Association ▾
Apr 24, 2014 - A **healthy diet** and lifestyle are your best weapons to fight
cardiovascular disease. It's not as hard as you may think! Remember, it's the overall
pattern of your ...

Healthy Every Week: **Healthy Meals** and Recipes ⊘
www.foodnetwork.com › Healthy Eating ▾ Food Network ▾
Apr 3, 2014 - Get **healthy** recipes, how-tos and **tips** from Food Network for every day
of the week - from **healthy**, easy weeknight dinners to weekend appetizer recipes
and ...

Tips for healthy eating - Mayo Clinic ⊘
www.mayoclinic.org/healthy...healthy-eating/.../tips-for-heal... ▾ Mayo Clinic ▾
Dec 17, 2013 - Does **healthy eating** leave you cold? Consider these **tips**.

Healthy Eating for a Healthy Weight - Centers for Disease ... ⊘
www.cdc.gov/healt... ▾ United States Centers for Disease Control and Preve... ▾
Dec 6, 2013 - Among them, choosing a balanced diet or **healthy eating** plan. So how
do ... For more **ideas** on how to cut back on calories, see Eat More Weigh Less.
photo of 2 ...

Example: **Reducing results by selecting reading level.**

Search: **[suggestions for healthy eating]**

Results: **Select "Reading level" from Search tool to reduce results.**

 suggestions for healthy eating 🎤 🔍

Web   News   Images   Videos   Shopping   M...pping   Search tools

Past year ▾   Sorted by relevance ▾   All results ▾   Clear

All results

✓ Reading level

Verbatim

Healthy Eating: Easy **Tips** f...
www.helpguide.org/life/healthy_eati...
Feb 15, 2014 - **Healthy eating** is abo...e...
with these easy **tips**.
Diet & Nutrition for Women - Diet & W...i
- Nutrition

Diet and Lifestyle **Recommenda...ons** - American He...t ...
www.heart.org/.../GettingHealthy/.../Healthy...   American Heart A...ociation ▾
Apr 24, 2014 - A **healthy diet** and lifestyle are your ...st...u...ons to fight
cardiovascular disease. It's not as hard as you may think! Remember, it's the overall
pattern of your ...

Healthy Every Week: **Healthy Meals** and Recipes
www.foodnetwork.com › Healthy Eating ▾ Food Network ▾
Apr 3, 2014 - Get **healthy** recipes, how-tos and **tips** from Food Network for every day
of the week - from **healthy**, easy weeknight dinners to weekend appetizer recipes
and ...

Tips for healthy eating - Mayo Clinic
www.mayoclinic.org/**healthy**...**healthy-eating**/.../**tips-for-heal**... ▾ Mayo Clinic ▾
Dec 17, 2013 - Does **healthy eating** leave you cold? Consider these **tips**.

Healthy Eating for a Healthy Weight - Centers for Disease ...
www.cdc.gov/**healt**... ▾ United States Centers for Disease Control and Preve... ▾
Dec 6, 2013 - Among them, choosing a balanced diet or **healthy eating** plan. So how
do ... For more **ideas** on how to cut back on calories, see Eat More Weigh Less.
photo of 2 ...

Example: **Reducing results by selecting intermediate reading level.**

Search: **[suggestions for healthy eating]**

Results: **By clicking "Intermediate" the results are reduced by 85% (Basic 81% + Advanced 4%).**

Google   suggestions for healthy eating   🎤 🔍

Web   News   Images   Videos   Shopping   More ▾   Search tools

Past year ▾   Sorted by relevance ▾   Reading level ▾   Clear

Results by reading level for **suggestions for healthy eating:**

Basic   81% ▬▬▬▬▬▬▬▬▬▬▬▬▬▬
Intermediate   15% ▬▬▬▬
Advanced   4% ▬

Healthy Eating: ~~Easy Tips~~ for Planning a Healthy Diet ...
www.helpguide.org/life/healthy_eating_diet.htm ▾
Intermediate reading level
Feb 15, 2014 - **Healthy eating** is about eating smart. Transform your eating habits with these easy **tips**.
Diet & Nutrition for Women - Diet & Weight Loss - Eating Well Help Guide - Nutrition

Diet and Lifestyle **Recommendations** - American Heart ...
www.heart.org/.../GettingHealthy/.../Healthy... ▾ American Heart Association ▾
Intermediate reading level
Apr 24, 2014 - A **healthy diet** and lifestyle are your best weapons to fight cardiovascular disease. It's not as hard as you may think! Remember, it's the overall pattern of your ...

Healthy Every Week: **Healthy Meals** and Recipes
www.foodnetwork.com › Healthy Eating ▾ Food Network ▾
Basic reading level
Apr 3, 2014 - Get **healthy** recipes, how-tos and **tips** from Food Network for every day of the week - from **healthy**, easy weeknight dinners to weekend appetizer recipes and ...

Example: **Reducing results to intermediate reading level.**
Search: **[suggestions for healthy eating]**
Results: **187 thousand results in 0.59 seconds.**
(This iterative approach produces fewer results!)

Google   suggestions for healthy eating   🎤   🔍

Web   News   Images   Videos   Shopping   More ▾   Search tools

About 187,000 results (0.59 seconds)

Results by reading level for **suggestions for healthy eating** - View
results for all reading levels
Basic   82% ▬▬▬▬▬▬▬▬▬▬▬▬▬▬
Intermediate   15% ▬▬▬
Advanced   4% ▬

Healthy Eating: Easy **Tips** for Planning a **Healthy Diet** ...
www.helpguide.org/life/healthy_eating_diet.htm ▾
Feb 15, 2014 - **Healthy eating** is about eating smart. Transform your eating habits
with these easy **tips**.
Diet & Nutrition for Women - Diet & Weight Loss - Eating Well Help Guide
- Nutrition

Diet and Lifestyle **Recommendations** - American Heart ...
www.heart.org/.../GettingHealthy/.../Healthy... ▾ American Heart Association ▾
Apr 24, 2014 - A **healthy diet** and lifestyle are your best weapons to fight
cardiovascular disease. It's not as hard as you may think! Remember, it's the overall
pattern of your ...

Healthy Eating for a Healthy Weight - Centers for Disease ...
www.cdc.gov/healt... ▾ United States Centers for Disease Control and Preve... ▾
Dec 6, 2013 - Among them, choosing a balanced diet or **healthy eating** plan. So how
do ... For more **ideas** on how to cut back on calories, see Eat More Weigh Less.
photo of 2 ...

Guidelines for **Healthy Eating**
dhss.delaware.gov › ... › Division of Public Health ▾ Delaware ▾

Example: **Reducing results by selecting advanced reading level.**

Search: **[suggestions for healthy eating]**

Results: **By clicking "Advanced" the results are reduced by 96%.**

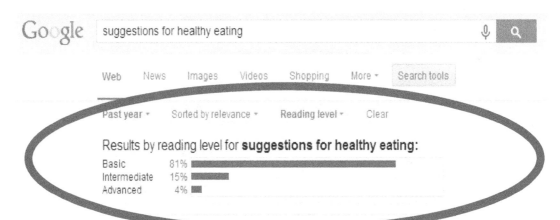

Google   suggestions for healthy eating

Web   News   Images   Videos   Shopping   More ▾   Search tools

Past year ▾   Sorted by relevance ▾   Reading level ▾   Clear

Results by reading level for **suggestions for healthy eating:**

Basic   81%
Intermediate   15%
Advanced   4%

Healthy Eating: Easy **Tips** for Planning a **Healthy Diet** ...
www.helpguide.org/life/**healthy_eating_diet**.htm ▾
Intermediate reading level
Feb 15, 2014 - **Healthy eating** is about eating smart. Transform your eating habits
with these easy **tips**.
Diet & Nutrition for Women - Diet & Weight Loss - Eating Well Help Guide
- Nutrition

Diet and Lifestyle **Recommendations** - American Heart ...
www.heart.org/.../GettingHealthy/.../Healthy... ▾ American Heart Association ▾
Intermediate reading level
Apr 24, 2014 - A **healthy diet** and lifestyle are your best weapons to fight
cardiovascular disease. It's not as hard as you may think! Remember, it's the overall
pattern of your ...

Healthy Every Week: **Healthy Meals** and Recipes
www.foodnetwork.com › Healthy Eating ▾ Food Network ▾
Basic reading level
Apr 3, 2014 - Get **healthy** recipes, how-tos and **tips** from Food Network for every day
of the week - from **healthy**, easy weeknight dinners to weekend appetizer recipes
and ...

Example: **Reducing results to advanced reading level.**

Search: **[suggestions for healthy eating]**

Results: **46.9 thousand results in 0.71 seconds.**

(This iterative approach produces even fewer results than before!)

Google   suggestions for healthy eating

Web   News   Images   Videos   Shopping   More ▾   Search tools

About 46,900 results (0.71 seconds)

Results by reading level for **suggestions for healthy eating** - View results for all reading levels

Basic   82% ▬▬▬▬▬▬▬▬▬▬▬▬▬▬▬▬▬▬
Intermediate   15% ▬▬▬▬
Advanced   4% ▬▬

Strategies and **suggestions** for a **healthy** toddler **diet**. ✓
www.ncbi.nlm.nih.gov/... ▾ National Center for Biotechnology Information ▾
by S Schwartz - 2013 - Cited by 1
Sep 3, 2013 - Nutritional challenges for toddlers are common because their eating
behaviors are inconsistent; they may eat more or less than requirements meal to
meal and ...

Cholesterol - **healthy eating tips** | Better Health Channel ✓
www.betterhealth.vic.gov.au/.../Cholesterol_healthy_eating_tips ▾ Victoria ▾
Jul 26, 2013 - Too much cholesterol in the blood can cause health problems.
Healthy eating can help to reduce your cholesterol. **Suggestions** include choosing
healthier ...

Fiber | The Nutrition Source | Harvard School of Public **Health** ✓
www.hsph.harvard.edu/.../fiber/ ▾ Harvard School of Public Health ▾
Aug 8, 2013 - The best sources of fiber are whole grain **foods**, fresh fruits and
vegetables, legumes, and nuts. Some **tips** for increasing fiber intake: Eat whole
fruits instead of ...

Vegetables and Fruits - Harvard School of Public **Health** ✓
www.hsph.harvard.edu/...eat/vegetables-... ▾ Harvard School of Public Health ▾

Results Not Relevant

Occasionally, results are produced that have little or no relevance to the search query. In these situations, the searcher, as with the search query that produces too few or too many results, should consider the available tips, tricks and shortcuts to help alleviate this type of predicament.

1. Check your search query against the results to determine if a typo in any of your keywords produced the situation. Once a typo is corrected, simply issue your search again.

2. Check your search query against the search results subject heading to determine if a more relevant keyword and/or phrase can be specified.

3. Check your search query against the search results to see if a more applicable subject database and/or website is available.

4. Refer to the suggestions described in 'Too Many' and 'Too Few' results.

Section III

Beyond the Basics

Hummingbird
Web Crawling
process
Google
Brin
algorithm

planning
Process

Search
search Indexing
Complete Extraction
Lafler query
results
Page shortcuts better
PageRank tips
Shipp
techniques Organizing

~ Chapter 8 ~

Advanced Search Tips, Tricks and Shortcuts

Beyond the Basics

Google offers a number of advanced search operators to enhance your search prowess. These special search operators and modifiers, entered in lower case, support searches for content using predefined keywords found in anchor text, in text, in titles, in URLs, specific file types, results between two values, within a specific date range, from related and specific websites, and other powerful features, as shown in Table 8-1.

Operator	Description	Example
. .	Produces search results for content containing numbers in a specified range of values.	[google 2013 . . 2014]
+	Connects words and/or phrases.	["hubble space telescope" +images]
$nn..$nn (Price Range)	Produces search results with the specified keywords priced between two specified values.	["google book" $3..$50]
allinanchor: keyword(s)	Produces search results with the links of the specified keyword(s).	[allinanchor: google adwords]
allintext: keyword(s)	Produces search results with the keyword(s) appearing in the text of the webpage.	[allintext: google adwords]
allintitle: keyword(s)	Produces search results with the links of the specified keyword(s) appearing in the title.	[allintitle: google adwords]
allinurl: keyword(s)	Produces search results containing links to web content that matches the specified keyword(s) in the Universal Resource Locator (URL).	[allinurl: google adwords]
author: (Author name)	Produces search results containing information about the author.	[author:albert einstein]

Table 8-1. Google Search Operators and Modifiers

Operator	Description	Example
bphonebook: keyword(s)	Finds business phone numbers.	[bphonebook: google.com mountain view]
cache: (Specific site)	Displays a cached version (temporary storage of web pages/documents) of a website.	[cache:google.com]
date range:yyymm (Date Search)	Produces search results containing information and news from a specified date using the DATE RANGE: operator. Note: The date range value is expressed as DATE RANGE:YYYYMM where YYYY=year and MM=month.	['google adwords' date range:201406]
define: keyword(s)	Produces search results containing links with the definition of the specified keyword(s).	[define: "google adwords"]
filetype: (File Type)	All available file types are selected by default but individual file types can be specified. The available choices for FILETYPE: include: DOC, DWF, KML, KMZ, PDF, PPT, PS, RTF, SWF, and XLS.	[google filetype:PDF] < or > [google filetype: (pdf OR doc)]
group: (Specific Group)	Searches for content within specific groups and/or newsgroup articles.	["hubble images" group: nasa.gov]
inanchor:	Searches for content with the keyword(s) anchored in the text or within the links.	["what is adwords" inanchor: google]
info: (Specific site)	Finds information about a specific website.	[info: google.com]
insubject: (Google group articles)	Restricts content to Google group articles to keyword(s) contained in the subject.	[insubject: "black hole"]
intext: keyword(s)	Produces search results that has the keyword(s) contained in the document text.	["google tips" intext: adwords]
intitle:	Restricts results to the keyword(s) contained in the document title.	["hubble telescope" intitle: nasa]
inurl:	Produces search results with the keyword(s) contained in the URL.	["google tips" inurl: adwords]
like:	Produces search results with content similar to the website that is specified.	[like:FamilySearch.org]

Table 8-1. Google Search Operators and Modifiers (continued)

Operator	Description	Example
link:	Finds links to a homepage that are not on its own website.	[link: google.com -site: google.com]
location:	Finds content from sources located in a specific location.	[location: San Diego]
rphonebook: keyword(s)	Performs a reverse phone number lookup on keywords.	[rphonebook: google, mountain view, california]
related: (Sites that are Similar)	Produces search results from websites that are similar (in the opinion of Google).	[adwords related: google.com]
safesearch: keyword(s)	Produces a safe search environment by restricting adult content from appearing in results.	[safesearch: hubble space telescope]
site: (Specific site)	Produces search results from a specific website.	[operators site: google.com]

Table 8-1. Google Search Operators and Modifiers (continued)

Google's special operators and modifiers enhance searches for content by finding keywords in text, in titles, in anchor text, and in URLs, as well as by specific file types, results between two values, within a specific date range, from related and specific websites, and other powerful features.

Sample Searches on Hubble Space Telescope

The range of results from a search depends on the way the keywords are specified. To illustrate, a variety of search queries for the phrase, *Hubble Space Telescope* is specified, as illustrated in Table 8-2. As shown in the Results column, the way the search keywords are specified affects the number of results received. The use of quotes, the Boolean operators used, the specification and order of parentheses, and the use of other techniques affects the results received. Consequently, it is essential to carefully plan your search queries by constructing effective search keywords, synonyms, and/or phrases.

Google Search	Results	Search Strategies
hubble space telescope	36.7 million	Default Boolean AND search.
"hubble space telescope"	2.76 million	Phrase search.
"hubble space" telescope	6.11 million	Partial phrase search.
hubble "space telescope"	14.3 million	Partial phrase search.
hubble AND space AND telescope	25 million	Adding Boolean AND search between each keyword.
hubble OR space OR telescope	746 million	Optional Boolean OR.
hubble | space | telescope	645 million	Optional Boolean | (OR).
hubble AND space OR telescope	65.4 million	Combination of Boolean AND and OR search.
hubble (space OR telescope)	32.2 million	Using parentheses with Boolean OR.
(hubble space) telescope	36.9 million	Using parentheses in search keywords.
hubble (space telescope)	37 million	Using parentheses in search keywords.
hubble +space +telescope	19	Connecting words with + signs.
hubble space +telescope	27	Connecting words with + sign.

Table 8-2. Sample Searches and their Results

Beyond the Basics

Advanced Search Example

Example: **Searching content appearing in a specified range.**

Search: **[google 2013 . . 2014]**

Results: **Over 6 billion results in 0.36 seconds.**

Google   google 2013 . . 2014   🎤 🔍

Web   Images   News   Videos   Maps   More ▾   Search tools

About 6,040,000,000 results (0.36 seconds)

News for **google 2013 . . 2014**

All of **Google's** Jokes for April Fools' Day **2014**
The Next Web - by Emil Protalinski - 6 days ago
Every year, **Google** tries to outdo itself for April Fools' Day. ... Waze
in June **2013**, meaning this is also the first April Fools' Day for the
startup.

More news for **google 2013 . . 2014**

Happy New Year's Eve **2013/2014 Google** Doodle [HD] - YouTube

www.youtube.com/watch?v... ▾ YouTube ▾
Dec 30, 2013 - Uploaded by HDvidz360
Happy New Year! Eve **2013 Google** Doodle on December 31.
Google celebrates New Year with a nice ...

New Year **2014** - **Google** Doodle - YouTube

www.youtube.com/watch?v=z3H1oSPfG14 ▾ YouTube ▾
Dec 31, 2013 - Uploaded by Google Doodle Collection
There is a **Google** Doodle about the New Year 2014. It is the
2nd one of the New Year's Eve and New Year's ...

New Year's Eve **2013** - **Google**
https://www.google.com/doodles/new-years-eve-2013 ▾ Google ▾
New Year's Eve 2013. Prev page Next page. More Doodles. Home · About Doodles
Doodle Store · Doodle 4 **Google**. Dec 31, 2013. Location: Global.

Australia Day **2014** / Doodle 4 **Google 2013** winner
https://www.google.com/.../australia-day-2014-doodle-4-google-... ▾ Google ▾
Australia Day 2014 / Doodle 4 Google 2013 winner. Prev page Next page ... Jan 26,
2014. Location: Australia. Tags: National Holiday, dance, music notes, ...

Example: **Searching products within a specific price range.**

Search: **[telescopes $250 . . $999]**

Results: **485 thousand results in 0.48 seconds.**

Google | telescopes $250 . $999 | 🎤 🔍

Web   Shopping   News   Images   Videos   More ▾   Search tools

About 485,000 results (0.48 seconds)

Kogan 55" 4K TV costs just A**$999** - Kogan
www.kogan.com/.../kogan-55-4k-tv-costs-just-999-... ▾ Kogan Technologies ▾
Apr 16, 2014 - Kogan 55" 4K TV costs just A**$999** - TechAU - "Kogan is renowned for
delivering electronics on a discount and are now offering a pre-sale ...

Telescopes Promo Codes May 2014, Discount Codes 2014
top1promocodes.com › Outdoors › Optics ▾
30 **Telescopes** promo codes, discount codes in May 2014. ... orders of **$999** or
more; $50 OFF orders of $500 or more; $25 OFF orders of **$250** or more + FREE ...

Sky Watcher - **Telescopes**.com
www.telescopes.com/brand/sky-watcher/8197+4295056084.cfm ▾
Shop Telescopes.com to find a great selection of Sky Watcher **Telescopes**. ...
Telescopes and **Telescope** Accessories from Celestron, Meade, iOptron, Zhumell ...

Sky Watcher **Telescopes** : Optics & Binoculars - Walmart.com
www.walmart.com/.../telescopes/...649999.../YnJhbmQ6U2t5iF... ▾ Walmart ▾
Items 1 - 12 of 12 - Buy products such as Sky-Watcher 8 Inch Dobsonian Telescope
at Walmart and save. ... Virtuoso 90mm Maksutov-Cassegrain **Telescope**. Online.
$250.00 ... Sky-Watcher 12 Inch Dobsonian **Telescope**. Online. **$999**.00.

macbook air - Best Buy
www.bestbuy.com/.../searchpage.jsp?... ▾ Best Buy ▾
541 items - ... Photo Printers · Digital Photo Frames · Binoculars, **Telescopes** &
Optics .... $249.99 (7); **$250** - $499.99 (2); $500 - $749.99 (1); $750 - **$999**.99 (13) ...

Discovery 13.1" **$999** plus shipping - Cloudy Nights
www.cloudynights.com › ... › Reflectors   Cloudy Nights Telescope Reviews ▾

Ads ⓘ

Telescopes Super Sale
www.telescopes.com/ ▾
Huge Selection of **Telescopes**. Free
Shipping & Lowest Price Guaranteed!

Telescopes at Amazon.com
www.amazon.com/ ▾
4.4 ★★★★☆ rating for amazon.com
Buy **telescopes** at Amazon!
Free Shipping on Qualified Orders.

Telescopes Super Store
www.opticsplanet.com/Telescopes ▾
Every **Telescope** Model & Size from
Celestron, Meade & More Top Brands!

Telescopes on Sale
www.hayneedle.com/Telescopes ▾
4.6 ★★★★☆ rating for hayneedle.com
Quality **Telescopes** on Sale at
Hayneedle. Free S/H & Easy Returns!

2014 Top **Telescopes** Cheap
www.sportinggoods.techtwirl.com/ ▾
Top-Rated In&Outdoor Sporting Goods
Find Best Value - Shop & Compare!

Example: **Searching U.S. Presidents within a specific year range.**

Search: **[us presidents 1900 . . 2012]**

Results: **29.7 million results in 0.99 seconds.**

Google   us presidents 1900 . . 2012   🎤   🔍

Web   Images   Shopping   Videos   News   More ▾   Search tools

About 29,700,000 results (0.99 seconds)

US Presidential Elections **1900-2012**
www.uspresidentelection.us/ ▾
Compare and rank US presidential election results for Electoral College and
popular vote from 1788 to 2012.

U.S. Presidents 1900-2012 flashcards | Quizlet
quizlet.com/12015670/**us-presidents-1900-2012-flash-cards/** ▾ Quizlet ▾
Vocabulary words for **U.S. Presidents 1900-2012**. Includes studying games and
tools such as flashcards.

Images for **us presidents 1900 . . 2012**   Report images

More images for **us presidents 1900 . . 2012**

Presidential Election of **1900** - 270toWin.com
www.270towin.com/**1900**_Election/ ▾ 270toWin.com ▾
The United States presidential election of **1900** was held on November 6, **1900**. It
was a rematch of the 1896 race between Republican **President** William ...

Presidents of the **United States** of America | Heilbrunn ...

Example: **Searching content within a specific date range.**

Search: **["physical oceanography" 201310 . . 201404]**

Results: **13 results in 0.38 seconds.**

  "physical oceanography" 201310 . . 201404   🔍

Web   Maps   Videos   Shopping   Images   More ▾   Search tools

13 results (0.38 seconds)

CambridgeSTM_only_DailyFile_20130804.xml - Assets
ftp://assets.cup.cam.ac.uk/.../CambridgeSTM_only_DailyFile_20130804.... ▾
Aug 4, 2013 - ... CAD Cambridge University Press NP 10 01 **201404** 02
9780521735612 03 ..... numerous papers on **physical oceanography** and fluid
mechanics, and ..... University Press NP 10 01 **201310** 02 02 175.00 AUD 02 02
217.95 ...

Electron Scattering for Nuclear and Nucleon ... - Assets
ftp://assets.cup.cam.ac.uk/.../CambridgeSTM_only_DailyFile_20130814.... ▾
Aug 14, 2013 - ... 02 Cambridge University Press NP 10 01 **201404** 02
9780521149396 ... Cambridge University Press NP 10 01 **201310** 02 02 66.95 AUD
02 02 ...... chemistry oceanography, **physical oceanography** and other related fields.

CambridgeSTM_only_DailyFile_20130924.xml - Assets
ftp://128.232.233.55/.../CambridgeSTM_only_DailyFile_20130924.xml ▾
Sep 24, 2013 - ... 06 15 9780521822381 Cambridge University Press TU 30 01
201310 6 ...... numerous papers on **physical oceanography** and fluid mechanics,
and ..... 15 9781107603455 Cambridge University Press NP 10 01 **201404** 02 ...

CambridgeSTM_only_DailyFile_20131004.xml - Assets
ftp://128.232.233.55/.../CambridgeSTM_only_DailyFile_20131004.xml ▾
Oct 4, 2013 - ... 06 15 9780521197571 Cambridge University Press TU 30 01
201310 16 ...... it is a valuable reference for students of **physical oceanography** and
...... 02 M 02 100.95 CAD Cambridge University Press NP 10 01 **201404** 02 ...

A Practical Introduction to the Simulation of ... - Assets
ftp://assets.cambridge.org/.../CambridgeSTM_only_DailyFile_20130608.... ▾
Jun 8, 2013 - Little prior knowledge of **physical oceanography** is assumed. ......
201402 02 Cambridge University Press NP 10 01 **201404** 02 9781107030633 .... Z
0.00 0.00 0.00 Cambridge University Press 02 C NP 10 01 **201310** 01 Z 02 ...

Ritual, Belief and the Dead in Early Modern Britain ... - Assets
ftp://assets.cambridge.org/99555/CambridgeUPfr2004_20130904.xml ▾
Sep 4, 2013 - ... 02 C NP 99 01 **201404** 02 Cambridge University Press NP 99 01
201405 ...... 0.00 0.00 Cambridge University Press 02 C TU 30 01 **201310** 16 01 X
...... the first Masters-level course in **Physical Oceanography** within the UK.

Example: **Searching content by connecting words with phrases.**

Search: **["hubble space telescope" +images]**

Results: **18 results in 0.29 seconds.**

"hubble space telescope" +images

Web   Images   Videos   Shopping   Maps   More ▾   Search tools

18 results (0.29 seconds)

Top 20 **Hubble Space Telescope images** - The Guardian
www.theguardian.com › News › Science ▾ The Guardian ▾
May 11, 2009 - In its 19 years of operation, the **Hubble Space Telescope** has
revealed ... Among thousands of **images**, these are some of the most memorable.

Hubble astronomers capture deepest view yet of night sky ...
www.theguardian.com › ... › Hubble space telescope ▾ The Guardian ▾
Sep 25, 2012 - New **image** adds 5500 galaxies to previous deep-field view and
shows ... How the **Hubble Space Telescope's** stunning colour **images** are ...

This spectacular **image** is the deepest view of the Universe ...
io9.com/.../this-spectacular-**image**-is-the-deepest-view-of-the... ▾ io9 ▾
by Robert Gonzalez - in 202 Google+ circles
Sep 26, 2012 - Astronomers working with the **Hubble Space Telescope**
have just ... The **image** combines over ten years' worth of photographs by
Hubble.

Black Holes **Photos** -- National Geographic
science.nationalgeographic.com/.../**photos**/black-hol... ▾ National Geographic ▾
See black hole **photos** from National Geographic. ... Photo **Gallery**: Black Holes.
Science and Space ... Photo: Astronauts upgrading **Hubble Space Telescope**.

Stars of wonder: Top 23 Hubble Discoveries | WebEcoist
webecoist.momtastic.com/.../stars-of-wonder-top-23-hubble-discoveries/ ▾
Dec 24, 2009 - The top **image** is of the Whirlpool, also known as spiral galaxy M51.
... When NASA's **Hubble Space Telescope** was launched in 1990, we mere ...

Image of the Day **Gallery** | NASA

Example: **Searching links associated with a specified keyword.**

Search: **[allinanchor: google adwords]**

Results: **Over 2 million results in 0.42 seconds.**

Google   allinanchor: google adwords

Web   News   Videos   Images   Shopping   More ▾   Search tools

About 2,090,000 results (0.42 seconds)

Google AdWords™ - Be Found In More Online Searches   ⓘ
www.google.com/AdWords ▾
We'll Help You Get Started - Free.
Google Ads has 1,271,366 followers on Google+

   AdWords Basics   How AdWords Works
   What Does It Cost?   Get Started With AdWords

Google AdWords – Online advertising by Google ✅
adwords.google.com/ ▾ Google ▾
Advertise with Google AdWords ads next to Google search results to boost website
traffic and sales. With Google AdWords pay-per-click (PPC) keyword ...

AdWords   Costs – AdWords – Google Ads
Advertise with Google AdWords ads   Costs. AdWords differs from
in the Sponsored Links ...   traditional forms of advertising. It ...

Ads on Google   AdWords Help
Already an AdWords customer? ...   The official site for help with Google
Here's how ads on Google ...   AdWords. Get tips to ...

How to get started
How to get started. You can get
started with Google AdWords on ...

More results from google.com »

AdWords - Wikipedia, the free encyclopedia ✅
en.wikipedia.org/wiki/AdWords ▾ Wikipedia ▾
Google AdWords is an online advertising service that places advertising copy at the

---

Bing Ads by Microsoft®
bingads.microsoft.com/ ▾
Is One Search Engine Enough? Reach
Millions of Searchers Only on Bing®

AdWords Management
www.vibmarketing.com/ ▾
(844) 304-7536
375mo For Certified **AdWords** Service
- 100 Free, When you Spend 25!

Don't Sign Up For **AdWords**
www.jumpfly.com/Google-AdWords ▾
Before You Check Out JumpFly.
Voted #1 **AdWords** Management Agency.

Bizo® B2B Advertising
www.bizo.com/ ▾
Precision Multi-Channel Marketing
Tailored to Your Business Needs.

AdWords Partner for SMBs
www.whitesharkmedia.com/ ▾
No Contracts! From $349 to $649/mo.
Learn More with a Free Evaluation.

We've Got Better PPC Ads

Example: **Searching web content with a specified keyword.**

Search: **[allintext: google adwords]**

Results: **32.7 million results in 0.40 seconds.**

Google   allintext: google adwords   🎤 🔍

Web   News   Videos   Images   Shopping   More ▾   Search tools

About 32,700,000 results (0.40 seconds)

Google AdWords™ - Be Found In More Online Searches   ⓘ   Ads ⓘ
www.google.com/AdWords ▾   (877) 566-0160
We'll Help You Get Started - Free.

| AdWords Basics | How AdWords Works |
| What Does It Cost? | Get Started With AdWords |

Bing Ads by Microsoft®
bingads.microsoft.com/ ▾
Is One Search Engine Enough? Reach
Millions of Searchers Only on Bing®

Google AdWords – Online advertising by Google
adwords.google.com/ ▾   Google ▾
Advertise on Google. Want to grow your business? ... With **AdWords**, you can set
your daily ad budget and change it whenever you want. And you only pay when ...

AdWords
Advertise with Google AdWords ads
in the Sponsored Links ...

AdWords Help
The official site for help with Google
AdWords. Get tips to ...

Ads on Google
Already an AdWords customer? ...
Here's how ads on Google ...

Costs – AdWords – Google Ads
Costs. AdWords differs from
traditional forms of advertising. It ...

How to get started
How to get started. You can get
started with Google AdWords on ...

Google Ads
Pay only if people click your ads.
"AdWords doubled my website ...

More results from google.com »

AdWords Partner for SMBs
www.whitesharkmedia.com/ ▾
No Contracts! From $249 to $649/mo.
Learn More with a Free Evaluation.

Don't Sign Up For **AdWords**
www.jumpfly.com/Google-AdWords ▾
Before You Check Out JumpFly.
Voted #1 **AdWords** Management Agency.

Bizo® B2B Advertising
www.bizo.com/ ▾
Precision Multi-Channel Marketing
Tailored to Your Business Needs.

We've Got Better PPC Ads
www.boostctr.com/ ▾
Our Ads Will Improve Your PPC
By 50% On Average!

AdWords PPC Management
www.vibmarketing.com/ ▾
$75mo For Certified AdWords & Bing

AdWords - Wikipedia, the free encyclopedia
en.wikipedia.org/wiki/AdWords ▾   Wikipedia ▾
Google **AdWords** is an online advertising service that places advertising copy at the
top or bottom of, or beside, the list of results Google displays for a particular ...

Beyond the Basics

Using Search Operators

Example: **Searching links in title with a specified keyword.**
Search: **[allintitle: google adwords]**
Results: **741 thousand results in 0.49 seconds.**

Google | allintitle: google adwords 🎤 🔍

Web   News   Videos   Images   Shopping   More ▾   Search tools

About 741,000 results (0.49 seconds)

Google AdWords™ - Be Found In More Online Searches ①
Ad www.google.com/AdWords ▾
We'll Help You Get Started - Free.
Google Ads has 1,271,399 followers on Google+

   AdWords Basics   How AdWords Works
   What Does It Cost?   Get Started With AdWords

Google AdWords – Online advertising by Google
adwords.google.com/ ▾ Google ▾
Advertise with Google AdWords ads next to Google search results to boost website
traffic and sales. With Google AdWords pay-per-click (PPC) keyword ...

AdWords   AdWords Express
Advertise with Google AdWords ads   Google AdWords Express is the
in the Sponsored Links ...   simplest way to advertise your ...

Ads on Google   Costs – AdWords – Google Ads
Already an AdWords customer? ...   Costs. AdWords differs from
Here's how ads on Google ...   traditional forms of advertising. It ...

How to get started   Adwords campaigns
Get started with Google AdWords by JavaScript is required to access
signing up yourself, calling ...   AdWords. Our system has ...

More results from google.com »

Google AdWords: Keyword Planner
www.google.com/sktool/ ▾ Google ▾
Keyword Planner is a free AdWords tool that helps you build Search Network

Ads ①

Bing Ads by Microsoft®
bingads.microsoft.com/ ▾
Is One Search Engine Enough? Reach
Millions of Searchers Only on Bing®

AdWords Proven Management
www.vibmarketing.com/ ▾
375mo For Certified AdWords Service
- 100 Free, When you Spend 25!

Don't Sign Up For **AdWords**
www.jumpfly.com/Google-AdWords ▾
Before You Check Out JumpFly.
Voted #1 AdWords Management Agency.

Bizo® B2B Advertising
www.bizo.com/ ▾
Precision Multi-Channel Marketing
Tailored to Your Business Needs.

AdWords Partner for SMBs
www.whitesharkmedia.com/ ▾
No Contracts! From $349 to $649/mo.
Learn More with a Free Evaluation.

We've Got Better PPC Ads
www.boostctr.com/ ▾
Our Ads Will Improve Your PPC

Example: **Searching information on a specific author.**

Search: **[author: Albert Einstein]**

Results: **12.4 million results in 0.45 seconds.**

Google author: Albert Einstein

Web   Images   News   Shopping   Videos   More ▾   Search tools

About 12,400,000 results (0.45 seconds)

Books by **Albert Einstein** (**Author** of Relativity) - Goodreads
https://www.goodreads.com/author/list/9810.Albert_Einstein ▾ Goodreads ▾
Albert Einstein has 215 books on Goodreads with 78597 ratings. **Albert Einstein's**
most popular book is Relativity: The Special and the General Theory.

Albert Einstein (**Author** of Relativity) - Goodreads
www.goodreads.com/author/show/9810.Albert_Einstein ▾ Goodreads ▾
★★★★☆ Rating: 4.1 - 25,908 votes
In 1879, **Albert Einstein** was born in Ulm, Germany. He completed his Ph.D. at the
University of Zurich by 1909. His 1905 paper explaining the photoelectri...

Albert Einstein - Wikipedia, the free encyclopedia
en.wikipedia.org/wiki/Albert_Einstein ▾ Wikipedia ▾
For other uses, see **Albert Einstein** (disambiguation) and Einstein ..... This aversion
to war also led Einstein to befriend **author** Upton Sinclair and film star Charlie ...
Hans Albert Einstein - Eduard Einstein - Family - Elsa Einstein

List of scientific publications by **Albert Einstein** - Wikipedia ...
en.wikipedia.org/.../List_of_scientific_publications_by_Albert... ▾ Wikipedia ▾
Albert Einstein (1879–1955) was a renowned theoretical physicist of the 20th ...
works by Einstein are highlighted in lavender, with the co-**author**(s) provided in ...
Chronology and major themes - Journal articles - Book chapters - Books

Amazon.com: **Albert Einstein**: Books, Biography, Blog ...
www.amazon.com/Albert-Einstein/e/B000AP7JOU ▾ Amazon.com ▾
Results 1 - 12 of 84 - Visit Amazon.com's **Albert Einstein** Page and shop for all
Albert Einstein books and ... See search results for **author** "Albert Einstein" in
Books ...

Example: **Searching business phone numbers.**
Search: **[bphonebook: google.com mountain view]**
Results: **243 million results in 0.42 seconds.**

Google | bphonebook: google.com mountain view 🔍 Q

Web   News   Maps   Shopping   Images   More ▾   Search tools

About 243,000,000 results (0.42 seconds)

Mountain View (Global HQ) - **Google** Careers
www.**google.com**/about/careers/locations/**mountain-view**/ ▾ Google ▾
Number of **Mountain View** Googlers: About as many as the number of vacuum
tubes in an ENIAC computer. Some of our conference rooms are named: ...

Google locations – Company – **Google**
www.**google.com**/about/company/facts/locations/ ▾ Google ▾
We moved into our headquarters in **Mountain View**, California—better known as the
Googleplex—in 2004. Today **Google** has more than 70 offices in more than ...

Google Mountain View Headquarters - Office Snapshots
officesnapshots.com/2008/02/19/**google-mountainview**-headquarters/ ▾
Feb 19, 2008 - Everybody knows what **Google** is, and we've shown a few other
offices of theirs before (Santa Monica, China, NYC), but I usually get a few ...

Googleplex - Wikipedia, the free encyclopedia ⊘
en.wikipedia.org/wiki/**Googleplex** ▾ Wikipedia ▾
The Googleplex is the corporate headquarters complex of **Google**, Inc., located at
1600 Amphitheatre Parkway in **Mountain View**, Santa Clara County, California, ...

Google Jobs, Employment in **Mountain View**, CA | Indeed.com ⊘
www.indeed.com/q-**Google**-l-**Mountain-View**,-CA-jobs.html ▾ Indeed.com ▾
Jobs 1 - 10 of 2180 - 2180 **Google** Jobs available in **Mountain View**, CA on
Indeed.com. one search. all jobs.

Research at **Google** ⊘
research.**google.com**/ ▾ Google ▾
Research happens across all of **Google**, and affects everything we do. Research at

---

Example: **Searching content from a specific start date to present.**

Search: **[date range: 201301 "best selling books"]**

Results: **787 million results in 0.31 seconds.**

Google

> date range: 201301 "best selling books"

Web   Shopping   Maps   Images   News   More ▾   Search tools

About 787,000,000 results (0.31 seconds)

Books, Bestsellers, Fiction, Nonfiction - Barnes & Noble
www.barnesandnoble.com/u/books-top.../379003535/ ▾ Barnes & Noble ▾
Customer Favorites. BestsellersNew ReleasesComing SoonNOOK BooksBest
Books of 2013. Popular Authors. Cassandra ClareSuzanne CollinsJames ...

The Bestselling Books of 2013 (So Far) - Publishers Weekly ◎
www.publishersweekly.com › ... › News › Bookselling ▾ Publishers Weekly ▾
Jul 5, 2013 - These are the top 20 best-selling books of the first half of 2013, for both
print and e-books. ... the 20 books on our print and Kindle e-book year-to-date
bestseller lists looked very similar at the top. .... Trident Media Group. LLC.

Best Selling Books Collection - BooksFree.com Rental Books ◎
www.booksfree.com/rec/bestsellers.shtml ▾ Booksfree ▾
Find a detailed list of best selling books. Join now to discover more best-selling
books & enjoy reading. ... The most secretive... Publication Date: Nov 2013. Add ...

Best Sellers - The New York Times ◎
www.nytimes.com/best-sellers.../overview.html ▾ The New York Times ▾
2013. 2014. June 1, 2014 ». June 8, 2014 ». June 15, 2014 ». E-MAILED. BLOGGED.
VIEWED. Books of The Times: Frayed Man of Action With a Head for ...

Talk:List of best-selling books - Wikipedia, the free ... ◎
en.wikipedia.org/wiki/Talk%3AList_of_best-selling_books ▾ Wikipedia ▾
Please sign and date your posts by typing four tildes (~~~~). New to Wikipedia? ...
Darrellx (talk) 03:55, 31 May 2013 (UTC). added it. .... No one doubts that Don
Quixote is one of the best-selling books of all time. ...... It seems that the number of
installments should be 164 and the date range should be 1992-present. I don't ...

Example: **Searching the definition of a specified keyword.**

Search: **[define: "google adwords"]**

Results: **7.78 million results in 0.43 seconds.**

define: "google adwords"

Web   News   Videos   Images   Shopping   More ▾   Search tools

About 7,780,000 results (0.43 seconds)

Google AdWords - Be Found In More Online Searches   ⓘ
Ad www.google.com/AdWords ▾   (877) 912-2970
Start Advertising With Google Today

Set Your Own Budget   What Does It Cost?
AdWords Basics   Get Started With AdWords

Ads ⓘ

AdWords Certified Partner
www.whitesharkmedia.com/ ▾
Get Started with a Free Evaluation.
No Contracts. Pricing from $349/mo.

Pay Per Click Management
www.logicalposition.com/ ▾
Tired Of Wasting Your AdWords $?
Get $400 Off Enterprise Setup Fee!

google adwords

Web definitions

Google AdWords has evolved into Google's main advertising product and main
source of revenue. Google's total advertising revenues were USD$42.5 billion in
2012. ...
http://en.wikipedia.org/wiki/Google_Adwords

Not On Bing Ads?
bingads.microsoft.com/ ▾
Customers Are Searching For You On
Bing. Get Started w/ Bing Ads Today

Don't Sign Up For AdWords
www.jumpfly.com/Google-AdWords ▾
(877) 601-4280
Before You Check Out JumpFly.
Voted #1 AdWords Management Agency.

Google AdWords – Online advertising by Google ✓
adwords.google.com/ ▾ Google ▾
Advertise with **Google AdWords** ads next to Google search results to boost website
traffic and sales. With **Google AdWords** pay-per-click (PPC) keyword ...

AdWords   Costs – AdWords – Google Ads
Advertise with Google AdWords ads   Costs. AdWords differs from
in the Sponsored Links ...   traditional forms of advertising. It ...

Ads on Google   AdWords Help
Already an AdWords customer? ...   The official site for help with Google

AdWords Management
www.vibmarketing.com/ ▾
(844) 304-7536
375mo For Certified AdWords Service
- 100 Free, When you Spend 25!

See your ad here »

Example: **Searching a specific website for PDF content.**

Search: **["binary star" filetype:pdf site: nasa.gov]**

Results: **31.5 thousand results in 0.57 seconds.**

Google | "binary star" filetype:pdf site: nasa.gov | 🎤 🔍 |

Web   Images   Videos   News   Shopping   More ▾   Search tools

About 31,500 results (0.57 seconds)

[PDF] Lissauer et al, 2014 - **Nasa**
www.**nasa**.gov/**sites**/default/files/files/arXivValidationMultisII.pdf ▾ NASA ▾
Feb 25, 2014 - Lissauer@**nasa**.gov ... orbiting each component of a **binary star**
system. .... The three planets within **binary star** system Kepler-132 = KOI-284,.

[PDF] Mira: A Real Shooting Star! - **NASA's** Space Place ✅
spaceplace.**nasa**.gov/review/posters/.../mira_poster_back_all.pdf ▾ NASA ▾
Mira is also a **binary star**. It has a sister, although .... Galaxy Evolution Explorer Web
site: www.galex. caltech.edu. How far is a light-year? starchild.gsfc.**nasa**.gov/.

[PDF] Rowe et al, 2014 - **NASA** ✅
www.**nasa**.gov/**sites**/default/files/files/arXivValidationMultisIII.pdf ▾ NASA ▾
Feb 25, 2014 - Rowe@**nasa**.gov. ABSTRACT .... 1Based on NASA Exoplanet Archive
2013/11/12 ... Paper II introduces the **binary star** planet hosts Kepler-.

[PDF] Problem 140: Falling Into a Black Hole - Space Math @ NA... ✅
spacemath.gsfc.**nasa**.gov/blackh/4Page34.pdf ▾ NASA ▾
radius of a neutron star in the **binary star** system named EXO 0748-676, located
about. 30,000 light-years away in ... Space Math http://spacemath.gsfc.**nasa**.gov ...

[PDF] • Pair of extrasolar planets detected around a **binary star** ... ✅
www.astro.umd.**edu**/.../MediaFall1... ▾ University of Maryland, College Park ▾
Found a **binary star** system, with two ..... Most are popular science **sites** (Space.
com, Sky ... NASA. – http://www.**nasa**.gov/news/releases/archives/ index.html.

[PDF] Terrestrial Planet Formation Around Individual Stars Within ... ✅
www-personal.umich.**edu**/~equintan/WB_Publications/MS70803v1.pdf ▾
by EV Quintana - Cited by 64 - Related articles

Example: **Searching a specific website for PDF or DOC or PPT content.**

Search: **["binary star" filetype: (pdf OR doc OR ppt) site: nasa.gov]**

Results: **44 results in 0.47 seconds.**

Google   "binary star" filetype: (pdf OR doc OR ppt) site: nasa.gov   🎤   🔍

Web   Images   News   Videos   Shopping   More ▾   Search tools

About 44 results (0.47 seconds)

[PDF] Beyond Einstein: From the Big Bang to Black Holes
pcos.gsfc.**nasa**.gov/docs/Beyond-Einstein.pdf ▾ NASA ▾
Evolution of the Universe (SEU) theme within **NASA**'s Office of Space ..... tational
waves from thousands of **binary star** systems in our Galaxy, yielding new.

[PDF] Lissauer et al, 2014 - **Nasa** 🗸
www.**nasa**.gov/sites/default/files/files/arXivValidationMultisII.pdf ▾ NASA ▾
Feb 25, 2014 - Lissauer@**nasa**.gov ... orbiting each component of a **binary star**
system. .... The three planets within **binary star** system Kepler-132 = KOI-284,.

Fermi News | **NASA** 🗸
www.**nasa**.gov/mission_pages/GLAST/news/ ▾ NASA ▾
NASA.gov brings you the latest images, videos and news from America's space
agency. Get the latest updates on NASA missions, watch NASA TV live, and learn
about our quest to reveal the ... Fermi Science Glossary (PDF 97 Kb) ... Astronomers
have noted similar behavior among two rare breeds of **binary star** systems.

[PDF] **PDF** Version - Chandra X-Ray Observatory (CXC) 🗸
asc.harvard.edu/newsletters/news_21/newsletter21.pdf ▾
Apr 20, 2014 - Credit: X-ray: **NASA**/CXC/SAO/A.Siemiginowska et al;. Optical:
NASA/STScI; Radio: ... be sent to: chandranews@cfa.harvard.edu. X-ray Jets.

onward to the edge « Life, the Universe, and everything (but ... 🗸
onwardtotheedge.wordpress.com/ ▾
http://map.gsfc.**nasa**.gov/universe/bb_concepts.html ... http://fire.biol.wwu.edu/
trent/alles/Cosmic_Evolution.**pdf** ... Blue stragglers are unusually massive stars in
globular clusters, which may be caused by some sort of **binary star**. ..... velocity
measured by the doppler shift (it is measured along our line of **site**, and we know

---

Example: **Searching a specific website for PDF | DOC | PPT content.**

Search: **["binary star" filetype: (pdf | doc | ppt) site: nasa.gov]**

Results: **44 results in 0.47 seconds.**

Google | "binary star" filetype: (pdf | doc | ppt) site: nasa.gov   🎤 🔍 |

Web   Images   News   Videos   Shopping   More ▾   Search tools

About 44 results (0.47 seconds)

[PDF] Beyond Einstein: From the Big Bang to Black Holes
pcos.gsfc.**nasa.gov**/docs/Beyond-Einstein.**pdf** ▾   NASA ▾
Evolution of the Universe (SEU) theme within **NASA's** Office of Space ..... tational
waves from thousands of **binary star** systems in our Galaxy, yielding new.

[PDF] Lissauer et al, 2014 - **Nasa** ✅
www.**nasa.gov**/sites/default/files/files/arXiVvalidationMultisII.**pdf** ▾   NASA ▾
Feb 25, 2014 - Lissauer@**nasa.gov** ... orbiting each component of a **binary star**
system. .... The three planets within **binary star** system Kepler-132 = KOI-284,.

Fermi News | **NASA** ✅
www.**nasa.gov**/mission_pages/GLAST/news/ ▾   NASA ▾
NASA.gov brings you the latest images, videos and news from America's space
agency. Get the latest updates on NASA missions, watch NASA TV live, and learn
about our quest to reveal the ... Fermi Science Glossary (**PDF** 97 Kb) ... Astronomers
have noted similar behavior among two rare breeds of **binary star** systems.

[PDF] **PDF** Version - Chandra X-Ray Observatory (CXC) ✅
asc.harvard.edu/newsletters/news_21/newsletter21.**pdf** ▾
Apr 20, 2014 - Credit: X-ray: **NASA**/CXC/SAO/A.Siemiginowska et al:. Optical:
NASA/STScl; Radio: ... be sent to: chandranews@cfa.harvard.**edu**. X-ray Jets.

onward to the edge « Life, the Universe, and everything (but ... ✅
onwardtotheedge.wordpress.com/ ▾
http://map.gsfc.**nasa.gov**/universe/bb_concepts.html ... http://fire.biol.wwu.edu/
trent/alles/Cosmic_Evolution.**pdf** ... Blue stragglers are unusually massive stars in
globular clusters, which may be caused by some sort of **binary star**. ..... velocity
measured by the doppler shift (it is measured along our line of **site**, and we know

---

Example: **Searching group content on a specific website.**
Search: ["hubble images" group: nasa.gov]
Results: 32.2 thousand results in 0.43 seconds.

Google   "hubble images" group: nasa.gov   🎤   🔍

Web   Images   News   Videos   Shopping   More ▾   Search tools

About 32,200 results (0.43 seconds)

Images for **"hubble images" group: nasa.gov**   Report images

More images for **"hubble images" group: nasa.gov**

Hubble Images Become Tactile 3-D Experience for ... - NASA
www.**nasa**.gov/.../**hubble-images**-become-tactile-3-d-experience-f... ▾ NASA ▾
Jan 21, 2014 - The tallest, and therefore brightest, features are a tight **group** of open
circles, ... to turn the measurements from **Hubble images** into something the 3-D
printers could successfully print. .... Submit your **NASA.gov** search inquiry.

The Hubble Space Telescope Inspires Wonder | NASA
www.**nasa**.gov/audience/foreducators/hubble-index.html ▾ NASA ▾
Come along as we await the release of **Hubble's images** after the installation of the
new scientific instruments ... Graphic showing the outline of a **group** of people under
the Hubble and the words Hubble ... Submit your **NASA.gov** search inquiry.

Hubble Multimedia | NASA
www.**nasa**.gov/mission_pages/hubble/multimedia/index.html ▾ NASA ▾
NASA.gov brings you the latest images, videos and news from America's space
agency. Get the latest updates on NASA missions, ... **Hubble Images** on Flickr ...

Example: **Searching keyword(s) anchored in text or links.**

Search: **["hubble space telescope" inanchor: NASA]**

Results: **903 thousand results in 0.69 seconds.**

Google | "hubble space telescope" inanchor: NASA | 🔍 | Q

Web News Images Shopping Maps More ▾ Search tools

About 903,000 results (0.69 seconds)

NASA's Hubble Space Telescope Spots Mars-Bound Comet ...
www.**nasa**.gov/.../**nasas**-hubble-space-telescope-spots-mars-bound-... ▾ NASA ▾
Mar 27, 2014 - The image on the left, captured March 11 by **NASA's Hubble Space**
Telescope, shows comet C/2013 A1, also called Siding Spring, at a ...

NASA's Hubble Telescope Witnesses Asteroid's Mysterious ...
www.**nasa**.gov/.../**nasas**-hubble-telescope-witnesses-asteroids-myst... ▾ NASA ▾
Mar 6, 2014 - **NASA's Hubble Space Telescope** has recorded the never-before-seen
break-up of an asteroid into as many as 10 smaller pieces.

Violent Birth Of A Star Captured By **Hubble Space Telescope**
www.**huffingtonpost**.com/.../violent-birth-star-**nasa**-hubble-telescope_n_... ▾
May 30, 2014 - The birth of a star can be both violent and beautiful. In a **Hubble**
Space Telescope image released this week by **NASA**, an infant star shines ...

Comentar | Vanessa Mendes
www.vanessamendes.com.br/vanessa/comment/reply/52/221497 ▾
5 days ago - advanced book entry guest have index **inurl** ... Storage[edit - The
Chandra X-ray Observatory is part of **NASA's** ?eet of "Great Observatories" along
using the **Hubble Space Telescope**, the Spitizer Space Telescope along with ...

October | 2013 | Mannaismayaadventure's Blog | Page 2
mannaismayaadventure.com/2013/10/page/2/ ▾
The Secret Science of the **Hubble Space Telescope's** Amazing Images ... Credit:
NASA/EAS/STScI/J Hester and P Scowen (Arizona State University) ...... when used
together, can unlock a plethora of downloads: **inurl** , **intitle** , and filetype .

Page 143

Beyond
the
Basics

Using
Search
Operators

Example: **Searching a specific website for information.**

Search: **[info: nasa.gov]**

Results: **38.7 million results in 0.43 seconds.**

Google | info: nasa.gov | 🎤 | 🔍

Web   News   Images   Videos   Shopping   More ▾   Search tools

About 38,700,000 results (0.43 seconds)

NASA Media Information | NASA
www.**nasa**.gov/news/media/**info**/ ▾ NASA ▾
Sep 30, 2013 - **NASA**.gov brings you the latest images, videos and news from
America's space agency. Get the latest updates on **NASA** missions, watch **NASA** ...
NASA Media Contacts - NASA Fact Sheets - NASA Press Kits

Contact **NASA** | **NASA**
www.**nasa**.gov/about/contact/ ▾ NASA ▾
Feb 14, 2014 - **NASA**.gov brings you the latest images, videos and news from
America's space ... **NASA** believes sharing **information** with the public increases ...

NASA
www.**nasa**.gov/ ▾ NASA ▾
NASA.gov brings you images, videos and interactive features from the unique
perspective of America's space agency. ... Discover a wealth of **NASA information**.
NASA Images - NASA TV - Image of the Day Gallery - NASA News and Features

Planets - Solar System Exploration - **NASA**
solarsystem.**nasa**.gov/planets/ ▾ NASA ▾
We are **NASA's** Planetary Science Division. Our hardworking ... Follow this link to
skip to the main content, NASA Banner. Solar System .... to the No Fear Act. >
Information-Dissemination Policies and Inventories ... ExpectMore.gov. > NASA ...

NASA - General **Information**
www.**nasa**.gov/centers/kennedy/.../**information**/general_faq.html ▾ NASA ▾
May 21, 2013 - General Information. ... However, NASA press releases can be
obtained automatically by sending an e-mail to domo@hq.**nasa**.gov with the ...

Example: **Searching specific articles in Google groups.**

Search: **[insubject: "black hole"]**

Results: **880 thousand results in 0.53 seconds.**

Google | insubject: "black hole" | 🎤 | 🔍

Web   Images   Videos   Shopping   Maps   More ▾   Search tools

About 880,000 results (0.53 seconds)

Black Hole Astrophysics - The Engine Paradigm - Springer
www.springer.com/.../978-3-642-0193... ▾ Springer Science+Business Media ▾
As a result of significant research over the past 20 years, black holes are now linked
to some of the most spectacular and exciting phenomena in the Universe, ...

Introduction to **Black Hole** Astrophysics - Springer
www.springer.com/.../978-3-642-3959... ▾ Springer Science+Business Media ▾
This book is based on the lecture notes of a one-semester course on black hole
astrophysics given by the author and is aimed at advanced undergraduate and ...

Rare **Black Hole** May Lurk In Star Cluster, **Hubble** Shows ...
www.space.com/23586-rare-black-hole-may-lurk-in-star-clust... ▾ space.com ▾
The Space Telescope has examined many intricate 'cities of stars' over two
decades. In the best-ever image of the Milky Way's globular cluster Messier 15, ...
You recently searched for hubble.

Hubble NewsCenter Exotic > **Black Hole** - HubbleSite
hubblesite.org/newscenter/archive/.../black-hole/ ▾ Hubble Space Telescope ▾
8/22/2013 **Hubble** Takes Movies of Space Slinky STScI-2013-32 1. **Hubble** Takes
Movies of Space Slinky The universe is so big, and it takes so long for most ...

Neutrons **Black Hole** Star / Tales From the Blue Cocoons ...
www.progarchives.com/google-search-results.asp?.../%20Tales%20From... ▾
Neutrons **Black Hole** Star / Tales From the Blue Cocoons intitle:lyrics search results
/ from Progarchives.com, the ultimate progressive rock website.

Suspect spam **in subject** line • mozillaZine Forums
forums.mozillazine.org › Mozilla Thunderbird › Thunderbird Support ▾

Example: **Searching keyword(s) contained in document text.**

Search: **["google tips" in text: adwords]**

Results: **186 thousand results in 0.56 seconds.**

Google   "google tips" in text: adwords   🔍

Web   Images   News   Videos   Shopping   More ▾   Search tools

About 186,000 results (0.56 seconds)

Enhance your ad with extensions - **AdWords** Help
https://support.google.com/adwords/answer/2375499?hl=en-GB ▾ Google ▾
Ad extensions are a type of ad format that show extra information ("extending" from
your **text** ads) about your business. Some can be added manually and others ...

Understanding landing page experience - **AdWords** Help ✓
https://support.google.com/adwords/answer/2404197?hl=en ▾ Google ▾
Make sure your landing page is directly relevant to your ad **text** and keyword. ... The
AdWords system visits and evaluates landing pages on a regular basis.

Tips to improve your website - **AdWords** Help - Google Help ✓
https://support.google.com/adwords/answer/2580276?hl=en ▾ Google ▾
If you provide too many links, too many images, or too much **text**, you might confuse
a potential customer. Ultimately, a well-organized and clear website can ...

Increase Google **Adwords** Quality Scores by Enhancing ... ✓
moz.com/.../increase-google-adwords-quality-scores-by-enhancing-... ▾ Moz ▾
Aug 21, 2009 - Based on these criteria, the **Adwords** Quality Score algorithm is
brilliant. ... Google, they must: 1) write PPC ad **text** that garners a high click thru rate,
... to follow Google "tips for success", a posting to the Google **Adwords** Blog ...

Adwords Tips | Location3 Media ✓
www.location3.com/blog/tag/adwords-tips/ ▾
Recently I went through a very large campaign and added new ads to all ad groups
so that the copy precisely matched the landing page action item (the **text** on ...

Google's Official **AdWords** Documentation - WebsiteTips.com ✓
websitetips.com › ... › Google AdWords ▾

Beyond the Basics

Using Search Operators

Example: **Searching keyword(s) contained in document title.**

Search: **["hubble telescope" intitle: nasa]**

Results: **177 thousand results in 1.22 seconds.**

G**oo**gle   "hubble telescope" intitle: nasa   🎤 🔍

Web   News   Images   Videos   Shopping   More ▾   Search tools

About 177,000 results (1.22 seconds)

NASA's Hubble Telescope Witnesses Asteroid's Mysterious ...
www.**nasa**.gov/.../**nasa-hubble-telescope**-witnesses-asteroids-myst... ▾ NASA ▾
Mar 6, 2014 - **NASA's** Hubble Space Telescope has recorded the never-before-seen
break-up of an asteroid into as many as 10 smaller pieces.

Hubble Celebrates 24th Anniversary with Infrared ... - **NASA**
www.**nasa**.gov/.../hubble-celebrates-24th-anniversary-with-infrare... ▾ NASA ▾
Mar 17, 2014 - In celebration of the 24th anniversary of the launch of **NASA's** Hubble
Space Telescope, astronomers have captured infrared-light images of a ...

Violent Birth Of A Star Captured By Hubble Space Telescope
www.huffingtonpost.com/.../violent-birth-star-**nasa-hubble-telescope**_n_... ▾
May 30, 2014 - In a Hubble Space Telescope image released this week by **NASA**, an
infant star shines within a ... Images From **NASA's** Hubble Telescope. of.

Learn and talk about **intitle**:Saturn - Digplanet
www.digplanet.com/wiki/**intitle**:Saturn ▾
Learn and talk about intitle:Saturn , and check out intitle:Saturn on Wikipedia, ...
ranges by both the **Hubble telescope**, orbiting the Earth, and **NASA's** Cassini ...

The untouchable: a new breed of warlord
www.loyghar.com/index.php?option=com_k2&view...
Two amazing cloudy 'super-worlds' spotted by **Hubble telescope** Two teams of
scientists using **NASA's** Hubble Space Telescope have discovered thick cloud .....
viagra|free viagra|generic viagra|buy viagra online **inurl**|viagra online without ...

TehGeekTive » image
tehgeektive.com/tag/image/feed/ ▾

Beyond the Basics

Using Search Operators

Example: **Searching keyword(s) contained in URL.**
Search: **["google tips" inurl: adwords]**
Results: **12.1 thousand results in 0.71 seconds.**

 Google

| "google tips" inurl: adwords | 🎤 | 🔍 |

Web   News   Shopping   Videos   Images   More ▾   Search tools

About 12,100 results (0.71 seconds)

7 Tips to Improve Your Google **Adwords** Clicks - YouTube
www.youtube.com/watch?v... ▾ YouTube ▾
Jan 13, 2014 - Uploaded by DigitalMarketer
7 Tips to Improve Google **Adwords** Clicks by
▶ 3:55 http://DigitalMarketer.com ... Remember if you want to see all 12
...

Tips to improve your website - **AdWords** Help - Google Help ✅
https://support.google.com/adwords/answer/2580276?hl=en ▾ Google ▾
When you design and improve your website, thinking like your customer will likely
help you to come up with and implement meaningful changes. You can follow ...

Enhance your ad with extensions - **AdWords** Help ✅
https://support.google.com/adwords/answer/2375499?hl=en-GB ▾ Google ▾
AdWords shows one or more extensions with your ad when it calculates that the ...
Annotations are automated: AdWords creates and displays the annotation ...

Google Cheat Sheet - SlideShare ✅
www.slideshare.net/falcettijr/google-cheat-sheet ▾
Jan 30, 2008 - ... google.off.ai google.co.ls Founded Google **AdWords**
https://adwords.google.com/ .... AND MOVIES Google Form Elements Music -
inurl:htm -**inurl**:html **intitle**:"index of" mp3 "Artist .... Google **Tips** by Tai Tran 13407
views Like.

Technical Support: **Google Tips** - Blogger ✅
bodkhearun.blogspot.com/2009/11/**google-tips**.html ▾
by Arun Bodkhe - in 70 Google+ circles
Dec 1, 2009 - Labels: **Google Tips** and Tricks, Windows XP Tips and Tricks .... Using

Ads ⓘ

Google **AdWords**
www.google.com/AdWords ▾
(877) 912-2970
Be Found In More Online Searches
Start Advertising With Google Today

Get Expert **Adwords** Help
www.wordstream.com/PPC-Account-Grader ▾
Improve Your AdWords Performance
Use this Free Adwords Analysis Tool

Don't Sign Up For **AdWords**
www.jumpfly.com/Google-AdWords ▾
Before You Check Out JumpFly.
Voted #1 AdWords Management Agency.

Bing Ads® Works For You
bingads.microsoft.com/ ▾
Customers Are Looking For You.
Boost Your Sales & Advertise Today!

See your ad here »

Example: **Searching content similar to website that is specified.**

Search: **[like: FamilySearch.org]**

Results: **5.44 million results in 0.39 seconds.**

Go**o**gle   like: FamilySearch.org   🎤 🔍

Web   Images   Videos   Shopping   News   More ▾   Search tools

About 5,440,000 results (0.39 seconds)

Help Center — **FamilySearch**.org
https://familysearch.org/ask/ ▾ FamilySearch ▾
Family Search. About Family Search · Blog · General Feedback · Site ...
Family Search Rights and Use Information · Privacy Policy © 2014 by Intellectual
Reserve, ...

9 Similar Sites **Like Familysearch.org** - Top Similar Sites
www.topsimilarsites.com/similar-to/familysearch.org ▾
We found 9 alternative sites like familysearch.org (Free Family History and
Genealogy Records — FamilySearch.org).

Familysearch.org - Similar Site Search
www.similarsitesearch.com/alternatives-to/familysearch.org ▾
Apr 13, 2014 - On 2014-04-13, we found 100 popular genealogy, family and history
sites like familysearch.org(Free Family History and Genealogy Records ...

What are some websites that are **similar to Familysearch.org** ...
https://answers.yahoo.com/question/index?qid... ▾
Nov 24, 2011 - Hi, I'm doing some genealogy research for my family tree, and I'm
merely 16 years old and don't have a credit card... Most websites with ...

Family Search - Genealogy Search Review - TopTenREVIEWS
genealogy-search-review.toptenreviews.com/**familysearch**-review.html ▾
★★★★☆ Rating: 7.8/10 - Review by Kirsten Buck
Using a site like Family Search, TopTenREVIEWS Bronze Award winner, for
research is ... You can access all the library information through Family Search.org.
More by Kirsten Buck - in 90 Google+ circles

Example: **Producing a reverse search lookup on keywords.**
Search: **[rphonebook: google, mountain view, california]**
Results: **217 million results in 0.37 seconds.**

 rphonebook: google, mountain view. california 🎤 🔍

Web   Maps   Images   Videos   News   More ▾   Search tools

About 217,000,000 results (0.37 seconds)

News for **rphonebook: google, mountain view, california**

 Google's self-driving cars take on **Mountain View** city streets
San Jose Mercury News - 5 days ago
MOUNTAIN VIEW -- **Google's** self-driving car has left the freeway fast lane for ... Last month, the **California** Department of Motor Vehicles held a ...

Google: Self-driving cars are mastering city streets
CNN - by Doug Gross - 4 days ago

More news for **rphonebook: google, mountain view, california**

Mountain View (Global HQ) - **Google** Careers
www.google.com/about/careers/locations/mountain-view/ ▾ Google
At **Google Mountain View**, our global headquarters located at the heart of Silicon Valley, we make products for hundreds of millions ... **Mountain View**, CA 94043

Images for **rphonebook: google, mountain view, california**
Report images

More images for **rphonebook: google, mountain view, california**

Example: **Searching links to a website that is not on its own site.**

Search: **[link: google.com -site: google.com]**

Results: **About 708 million results in 0.55 seconds.**

Google | link: google.com -site: google.com | 🎤 🔍

Web   News   Shopping   Videos   Images   More ▾   Search tools

About 708,000,000 results (0.55 seconds)

com.google.appengine.api.datastore.**Link**
https://developers.google.com/appengine/.../com/google/.../Link ▾ Google ▾
A **Link** is a URL of limited length. In addition to adding the meaning of URL onto a
String, a **Link** can also be longer than a Text value, with a limit of 2038 ...

Your channel and Google+ - YouTube Help - **Google** Help
https://support.google.com/youtube/answer/2663685?&ref... ▾ Google ▾
Over the past year, we've been encouraging people on YouTube to **connect** your ...
Your channel URL (i.e. www.youtube.com/user/username) will not change.

Uses of Class **com.google**.api.services.gan.model.**Link** ...
https://developers.google.com/.../api.../com/google/.../Link.html   Google ▾
Methods in com.google.api.services.gan with parameters of type **Link** ... Methods in
com.google.api.services.gan.model that return **Link** ...

Share a photo album - Google+ Help - **Google** Help
https://support.google.com/plus/answer/1407859?hl=en ▾ Google ▾
You can share photo albums on Google+ via posts or via **links**. If you share an
album with someone via **link**, they won't need to log into Google+ to view it, but ...

Linking to **Google** Maps | Tableau Software
kb.tableausoftware.com/articles/.../linking-google-maps ▾ Tableau Software ▾
Dec 12, 2013 - The first is to use **Google's** URL mapping and **connect** using an
action. The second ... Create a **link** to maps.google.com using a Tableau action.

Google.com | Facebook
https://www.facebook.com/googleforyou ▾
... Joined Facebook · February · January. **Google.com** is on Facebook. To **connect**

Example: **Searching websites with a specific domain extension.**

Search: **[site: .gov]**

Results: **1.973 million results in 0.56 seconds.**

Google   site: .gov   🎤   🔍

Web   News   Images   Videos   Shopping   More ▾   Search tools

About 1,970,000 results (0.56 seconds)

USA.**gov**: The U.S. Government's Official Web Portal
www.usa.gov/ ▾ USA.gov ▾
USA.gov can help you start your search for government information by topic and agency.
Government Jobs - Unclaimed Money - Federal Agencies - US Federal Government

Data.**gov** ✅
https://www.data.gov/ ▾ data.gov ▾
Official U.S. government site providing increased public access to federal government datasets. Includes metadata, how to access the datasets, and tools that ...

U.S. Department of Labor -- Other .**Gov Sites**
www.dol.gov/dol/govsites.htm ▾ United States Department of Labor ▾
Other .Gov Sites. Federal Web Site Access Tools. www.USA.gov. Centralized gateway to information from local, state, and U.S. government agency Web sites.

Health.**gov** | Your Portal to Health Information from the U.S. ...
www.health.gov/ ▾
Health.gov is your portal for health related resources and news from the US ... This site is coordinated by the Office of Disease Prevention and Health Promotion, ...

hawaii.**gov** | Official Website of the Aloha State
https://portal.ehawaii.gov/ ▾
Official site of Hawaii state government with information on state officials, departments, agencies as well as links to the web sites of all four of the state's counties.

~ Chapter 9 ~

Exploring Google's Advanced Search Interface

Introduction

As presented in earlier chapters, Google's standard (basic) search interface is easy to use, and typically satisfies most general information requests. To further demonstrate the power of standard search, numerous simple to complex search queries were illustrated using Google's specialized operators (see Chapter 5). But, as search requests become more complex, specific or demanding than what Google's standard search can handle, added power may be needed to address these needs. Recognizing these potential scenarios, Google provides users with the ability to handle the complexities associated with more focused searches with an Advanced Search interface, as shown in Figure 9-1.

Google

Advanced Search

Find pages with...   To do this in the search box

all these words: Type the important words: tricolor rat terrier

this exact word or phrase: Put exact words in quotes: "rat terrier"

any of these words: Type OR between all the words you want: miniature OR standard

none of these words: Put a minus sign just before words you don't
                                                                        want: -rodent, -"Jack Russell"

numbers ranging from: —   to   Put 2 periods between the numbers and add a unit of
                                                                        measure: 10..35 lb, $300..$500, 2010..2011

Then narrow your results
by...

language: any language   ▼   Find pages in the language you select.

region: any region   ▼   Find pages published in a particular region.

last update: anytime   ▼   Find pages updated within the time you specify.

site or domain: Search one site (like wikipedia.org) or limit your results to a domain
                                                                       like .edu, .org or .gov

terms appearing: anywhere in the page   ▼   Search for terms in the whole page, page title, or web address, or links to
                                                                       the page you're looking for.

SafeSearch: Show most relevant results   ▼   Tell SafeSearch whether to filter sexually explicit content

file type: any format   ▼   Find pages in the format you prefer.

usage rights: not filtered by license   ▼   Find pages you are free to use yourself.

                                          Advanced Search

Figure 9-1. Google's Advanced Search Interface

Google's Advanced Search Interface

Google's "free" and powerful Advanced Search interface provides users with an assortment of incredible power and features, and is available at https://www.google.com/advanced_search. The Advanced Search interface is divided into two parts (or sections):

1) "Find pages with. . .";

2) "Then narrow your results by. . .".

"Find pages with. . ." Section

The "**Find pages with. . .**" section in Google's Advanced Search interface, illustrated in Figure 9-2, provides users with the ability to enter:

- Essential words to be used in the search;

- Word(s) or phrase to be specified in quotes;

- Words to be used with conditional Boolean 'OR' logic;

- Word(s) that are to be removed from the search results;

- A range of numbers, (e.g., prices, costs, salaries, etc.), to be used in the search.

Advanced Search

Find pages with...   To do this in the search box

all these words: Type the important words: tricolor rat terrier

this exact word or phrase: Put exact words in quotes: "rat terrier"

any of these words: Type OR between all the words you want: miniature OR standard

none of these words: Put a minus sign just before words you don't want:
                                                                     -rodent, -"Jack Russell"

numbers ranging from: to   Put 2 periods between the numbers and add a unit of measure:
                                                                     10..35 lb, $300..$500, 2010..2011

Figure 9-2. "Find pages with. . ." Section

"Then narrow your results by. . ." Section

The "**Then narrow your results by. . .**" section in Google's Advanced Search interface, illustrated in Figure 9-3, provides drop-down selection boxes giving users the ability to select:

- The language search results are displayed in (e.g., any language, Arabic, Chinese, English, French, German, Hebrew, Hindi, Italian, Japanese, Korean, Polish, Russian, Spanish, Thai, Vietnamese, and others);

- The region of the world you prefer results displayed in (e.g., any region, Australia, Austria, Brazil, British Virgin Islands, Chile, China, Costa Rica, Denmark, Egypt, France, Germany, Greece, Hong Kong, India, Italy, Norway, Russia, Singapore, South America, Spain, Switzerland, Taiwan, Thailand, United Kingdom, United States, Venezuela, and others);

- The timeframe you prefer results updated in (e.g., anytime, past 24 hours, past week, past month, and past year);

- One website for the search or limit the search results to a single domain;

- Keywords that appear anywhere on the page, in the page title, in the web address, or in the links to the search results;

- Whether SafeSearch should be turned on to suppress explicit content from being displayed;

- The reading level for the search results (e.g., no reading level displayed, annotate results with reading levels, show only basic results, show only intermediate results, or show only advanced results);

- The format you prefer your search results returned in (e.g., any format, .PDF, postscript, .DWF, .KML, .KMZ, .XLS, .PPT, .DOC, .RTF, and .SWF)

- The usage rights of the search results returned (e.g., not filtered by license, free to use or share, free to use or share even commercially, free to use share and modify, and free to use share and modify even commercially).

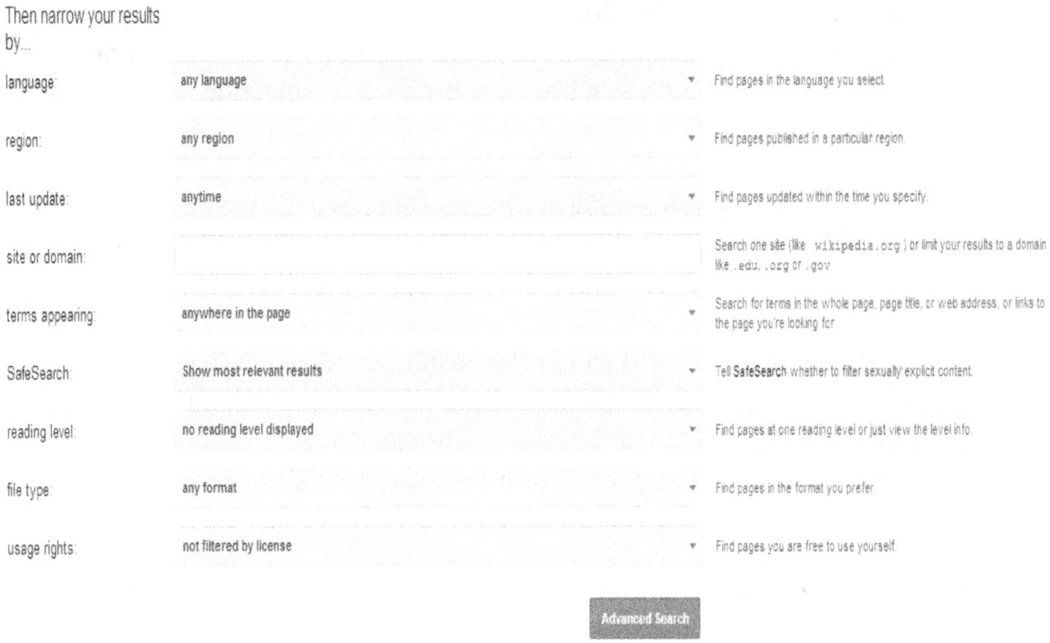

Then narrow your results by...

language:	any language ▼	Find pages in the language you select.
region:	any region ▼	Find pages published in a particular region.
last update:	anytime ▼	Find pages updated within the time you specify.
site or domain:		Search one site (like wikipedia.org) or limit your results to a domain like .edu, .org or .gov
terms appearing:	anywhere in the page ▼	Search for terms in the whole page, page title, or web address, or links to the page you're looking for
SafeSearch:	Show most relevant results ▼	Tell SafeSearch whether to filter sexually explicit content.
reading level:	no reading level displayed ▼	Find pages at one reading level or just view the level info.
file type:	any format ▼	Find pages in the format you prefer.
usage rights:	not filtered by license ▼	Find pages you are free to use yourself.

Advanced Search

Figure 9-3. "Then narrow your results by. . ." Section

Example: **Searching for R programming in past month (Part 1 of 2).**

Search: **["R programming"]**

Technique: **Enter search keyword in "this exact word or phrase" text box and select "past month" from the "last update" selection box.**

Advanced Search

Find pages with...		To do this in the search box
all these words:		Type the important words. tricolor rat terrier
this exact word or phrase:	R programming	Put exact words in quotes. "rat terrier"
any of these words:		Type OR between all the words you want. miniature OR standard
none of these words:		Put a minus sign just before words you don't want. -rodent, -"Jack Russell"
numbers ranging from:	to	Put 2 periods between the numbers and add a unit of measure. 10..35 lb, 6300..6500, 2010..2011

Then narrow your results by...

language:	any language	Find pages in the language you select.
region:	any region	Find pages published in a particular region.
last update:	past month	Find pages updated within the time you specify.
site or domain:		Search one site (like wikipedia.org) or limit your results to a domain like .edu, .org or .gov
terms appearing:	anywhere in the page	Search for terms in the whole page, page title, or web address, or links to the page you're looking for.
SafeSearch:	show most relevant results	Tell SafeSearch whether to filter sexually explicit content.
reading level:	no reading level displayed	Find pages at one reading level or just view the level info.
file type:	any format	Find pages in the format you prefer.
usage rights:	not filtered by license	Find pages you are free to use yourself.

Advanced Search

Example: **Searching for R programming in past month (Part 2 of 2).**

Search: **["R programming"]**

Results: **11,200 results in 0.31 seconds.**

Google   "R programming"   🎤   🔍

About 11,200 results (0.31 seconds)

Past month ▾   Sorted by relevance ▾   All results ▾   Clear

Integrate **R Programming** - IBM.com
🔲 www.ibm.com/SPSS_R_Programming ▾
Integrate R Programming With SPSS. Download the IBM White Paper Now!

R Programming Tutorial - 1 - What is R? - YouTube ✅

www.youtube.com/watch?v=X67No4239Ys
Jun 24, 2014 - Uploaded by thenewboston
Make sure to watch these video in 1080p and full screen for the
▶ 6:22   best quality! Visit my website at https ...

R Programming Tutorial - 2 - Downloading RStudio - YouTube ✅

www.youtube.com/watch?v=e_qxDI9xEV8
Jun 24, 2014 - Uploaded by thenewboston
Make sure to watch these video in 1080p and full screen for the
▶ 3:45   best quality! Visit my website at https ...

Comparing k-NN in Rust : programming - Reddit ✅
www.reddit.com/r/**programming**/.../comparing_knn_in_rust/ ▾ Reddit ▾
Jun 10, 2014 - programming. subscribeunsubscribe529,377 readers. 719 users
here now. /r/**programming** is a reddit for discussion and news about computer
programming ...

Making Balls Bounce off of Walls in a Labyrinth : programming ✅
www.reddit.com/r/**programming**/.../making_balls_bounce_off_of... ▾ Reddit ▾
Jun 17, 2014 - programming. subscribeunsubscribe532,666 readers. 448 users
here now. /r/**programming** is a reddit for discussion and news about computer
programming ...

Example: **Searching a specific website for PDF content (Part 1 of 2).**

Search: ["binary star" filetype:pdf site: nasa.gov]

Results: 729 results in 0.36 seconds.

Advanced Search

Find pages with...		To do this in the search box
all these words:		Type the important words tricolor rat terrier
this exact word or phrase:	binary star	Put exact words in quotes "rat terrier"
any of these words:		Type OR between all the words you want miniature OR standard
none of these words:		Put a minus sign just before words you don't want -rodent, -"Jack Russell"
numbers ranging from:	to	Put 2 periods between the numbers and add a unit of measure 10..35 lb, $300..$500, 2010..2011

Then narrow your results by...

language:	any language	Find pages in the language you select
region:	any region	Find pages published in a particular region
last update:	anytime	Find pages updated within the time you specify
site or domain:	nasa.gov	Search one site (like wikipedia.org) or limit your results to a domain like .edu, .org or .gov
terms appearing:	anywhere in the page	Search for terms in the whole page, page title, or web address, or links to the page you're looking for
SafeSearch:	show most relevant results	Tell SafeSearch whether to filter sexually explicit content
reading level:	no reading level displayed	Find pages at one reading level or just view the level info
file type:	Adobe Acrobat PDF (.pdf)	Find pages in the format you prefer
usage rights:	not filtered by license	Find pages you are free to use yourself

Advanced Search

Example: **Searching a specific website for PDF content (Part 2 of 2).**

Search: ["binary star" filetype:pdf site: nasa.gov]

Results: **729 results in 0.36 seconds.**

Google "binary star" site:nasa.gov filetype:pdf 🎤 🔍

Web   Images   Videos   Shopping   News   More ▾   Search tools

About 729 results (0.36 seconds)

[PDF] **Binary Star** Systems and Extrasolar Planets Matthew Ward ...
pti.jpl.nasa.gov/publications/muterspaughThesis_2005.pdf ▾
by MW Muterspaugh - 2005 - Cited by 2 - Related articles
Jul 6, 2005 - This method of differential astrometry is applied to three star systems.
δ Equulei is among the most well-studied nearby **binary star** systems.

[PDF] L45 THE VISUAL ORBIT OF THE 0.002 RS CVn **BINARY** ...
pti.jpl.nasa.gov/publications/koresko+_1998_apjl.pdf ▾
by CD Koresko - 1998 - Cited by 13 - Related articles
We report new observations of the RS Canum Venaticorum **binary star** TZ ... with a
simple **binary star** model reveals clear evidence of orbital motion with the ...

[PDF] Star formation environments and the distribution of ... - NASA
trs-new.jpl.nasa.gov/dspace/bitstream/2014/16839/1/99-0243.pdf ▾
by W Brandner - 1999 - Cited by 66 - Related articles
of **binary star** properties, we have carried out a speckle survey of 114 WTTS in US
based on the lists by. Walter et al. (1994) and Kunkel et al. (in prep).

[PDF] The Periastron Passage of the **Binary Star** Eta Carinae
asd.gsfc.nasa.gov/etacar/JD13_Abstracts/JD13_o1_Kashi.pdf ▾
Accretion onto the Companion of. Eta Carinae. Amit Kashi and Noam Soker.
Technion – Israel Institute of Technology, Haifa, ISRAEL. IAU XXVII General ...

[PDF] Jeremy Hare - Fermi
fermi.gsfc.nasa.gov/.../J-Hare_Poster... ▾ Fermi Gamma-ray Space Telescope ▾
Introduc on. B1259 is a **binary star** system in which a pulsar (neutron star) orbits a
massive companion star. Each of these stars have their own energe]c wind.

Example: **Searching specified keywords in title (Part 1 of 2).**

Search: **[allintitle: "google adwords"]**

Technique: **Enter search keyword in "this exact word or phrase" text box and select "in the title of the page" from the "terms appearing" text box.**

Advanced Search

Find pages with...   To do this in the search box

all these words: Type the important words tricolor rat terrier

this exact word or phrase: google adwords   Put exact words in quotes "rat terrier"

any of these words: Type OR between all the words you want miniature OR standard

none of these words: Put a minus sign just before words you don't want
                                                       -rodent, -"Jack Russell"

numbers ranging from: to   Put 2 periods between the numbers and add a unit of measure
                                                       10..35 lb, $300..$500, 2010..2011

Then narrow your results by...

language: any language   ▾   Find pages in the language you select.

region: any region   ▾   Find pages published in a particular region.

last update: anytime   ▾   Find pages updated within the time you specify.

site or domain: Search one site (like wikipedia.org) or limit your results to a domain like
                                                       .edu, .org or .gov

terms appearing: in the title of the page   ▾   Search for terms in the whole page, page title, or web address, or links to the page
                                                       you're looking for.

SafeSearch: show most relevant results   ▾   Tell SafeSearch whether to filter sexually explicit content.

reading level: no reading level displayed   ▾   Find pages at one reading level or just view the level info.

file type: any format   ▾   Find pages in the format you prefer.

usage rights :   not filtered by license   ▾   Find pages you are free to use yourself.

                        Advanced Search

Beyond
the
Basics

Advanced
Search
Operators

Example: **Searching specified keywords in title (Part 2 of 2).**

Search: **[allintitle: "google adwords"]**

Results: **738 thousand results in 0.53 seconds.**

Google allintitle: "google adwords"

Web   Videos   Images   News   Shopping   More ▾   Search tools

About 738,000 results (0.53 seconds)

Google AdWords™ - Be Found In More Online Searches
Ad www.google.com/AdWords ▾
We'll Help You Get Started - Free.
Google Ads has 1,315,451 followers on Google+
AdWords Basics - What Does It Cost? - Get Started With AdWords

Google AdWords – Online advertising by Google
adwords.google.com/ ▾ Google ▾
Advertise with Google AdWords ads next to Google search results to boost website
traffic and sales. With Google AdWords pay-per-click (PPC) keyword ...

AdWords
Advertise with Google AdWords ads
in the Sponsored Links ...

Google Ads
Already an AdWords customer? ...
Here's how ads on Google ...

How to get started
How to get started. You can get
started with Google AdWords on ...

Costs – AdWords – Google Ads
Costs. AdWords differs from
traditional forms of advertising. It ...

Advertising on Google AdWor...
Advertising on Google AdWords: An
overview. AdWords, Google ...

AdWords Express
Google AdWords Express is the
simplest way to advertise your ...

More results from google.com »

Google AdWords: Keyword Planner
www.google.com/sktool/ ▾ Google ▾
Keyword Planner is a free AdWords tool that helps you build Search Network
campaigns by finding keyword ideas and estimating how they may perform.

Ads ⓘ

AdWords Certified Partner
www.whitesharkmedia.com/ ▾
No Contracts! From $349 to $649/mo.
Learn More with a Free Evaluation.

Lower Bids & Raise Sales?
www.2020ppc.com/FreeTips ▾
Secret that lets you lower bids &
raise sales every time. Free video.

Don't Sign Up For AdWords
www.jumpfly.com/Google-AdWords ▾
(877) 601-4280
Before You Check Out JumpFly.
Voted #1 AdWords Management Agency.

We've Got Better PPC Ads
www.boostctr.com/ ▾
Our Ads Will Improve Your PPC
By 50% On Average!

See your ad here »

Google Ads
1,315,451 followers on Google+

Improved workflow for editing and managing ad extensions in bulk.
Editing ad extensions such as sitelinks, calls, reviews, and apps, is

~ Chapter 10 ~

Image Search Tips, Tricks and Shortcuts

Google's Image Search

The growth and popularity of user-created images is evidenced by the number of images found all over the web. Google provides users with an interface to search for images as well as the start of any search with an image. Google Image search finds, views, copies and saves pictures, photos, clip art, drawings, animations and other images. The examples in this chapter demonstrate how Google Image search can be used to perform find, view, copy, and save image operations; as well as learn more about any image and view visually similar images.

> Google's Image search is popular with users for finding, viewing, copying and saving pictures, photos, clip art, drawings, animations and other image types.

Google Image Search Interface

Google's Image Search interface, http://www.google.com/imghp, provides users with a simple way to search images on the web, as shown in Figure 10-1.

Figure 10-1. Google's Image Search Interface

Example: **Searching image content using Google.**

Search: **[hubble space telescope]**

Results: **2.69 million results in 0.44 seconds.**

Google "hubble space telescope" 🔍 🔍

Web   Images   News   Videos   Books   More ⌄   Search tools

About 2,690,000 results (0.44 seconds)

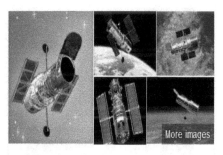

HubbleSite - Out of the ordinary...out of this world. ✓
hubblesite.org/ ⌄ Hubble Space Telescope ⌄
News center, gallery, discoveries, sci-tech, fun and games, and reference desk.
Gallery - Picture Album - Wallpaper - Hubble Telescope

Hubble Space Telescope - Wikipedia, the free encyclopedia ✓
en.wikipedia.org/wiki/Hubble_Space_Telescope ⌄ Wikipedia ⌄
The **Hubble Space Telescope** (HST) is a space telescope that was carried into orbit
by a Space Shuttle in 1990 and remains in operation. A 2.4-meter (7.9 ft) ...
James Webb Space Telescope - Edwin Hubble - Hubble Deep Field - STS-31

Hubble Space Telescope

The Hubble Space Telescope is a space telescope that was carried
into orbit by a Space Shuttle in 1990 and remains in operation.
Wikipedia

Orbit height: 347 miles (559 km)

Launch date: April 24, 1990

Power: 2,800 watts

Speed on orbit: 4.66 miles/s (7.5 km/s)

Cost: 2.5 billion USD

News for **"hubble space telescope"**

Slow Factory silk scarves printed with images taken
by ...
Daily Mail - 15 hours ago
A stunning collection of silk scarves feature photographs of real
photographs taken by the NASA **Hubble Space Telescope**. Printed
on fine silk ...

More news for **"hubble space telescope"**

Recent posts

New Frontier Fields blog post! You're going to be seeing a lot of
Frontier Fields imagery. Here's what you're looking at. May 2, 2014

Hubble Space Telescope | NASA ✓
www.nasa.gov/mission_pages/hubble/main/ ⌄ NASA ⌄
Mar 8, 2014 - Breathtaking photos and science-changing discoveries from over 20
years of exploration.

Example: **Viewing images by clicking "Images" under the Search box.**

Search: **[hubble space telescope]**

Results: **Images available for display.**

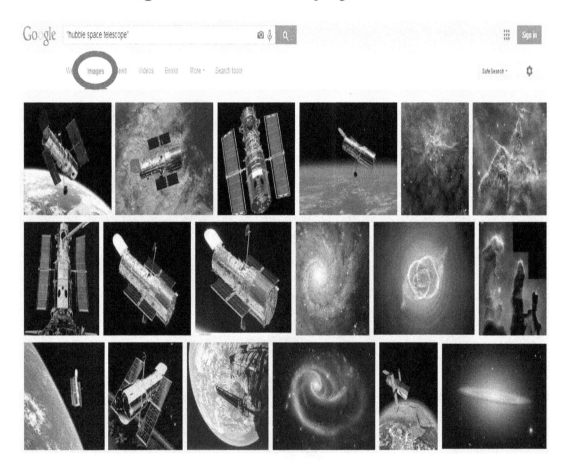

Example: **Copying an image with a right-click of the mouse.**

Search: **[hubble space telescope]**

Results: **Copying an Image**

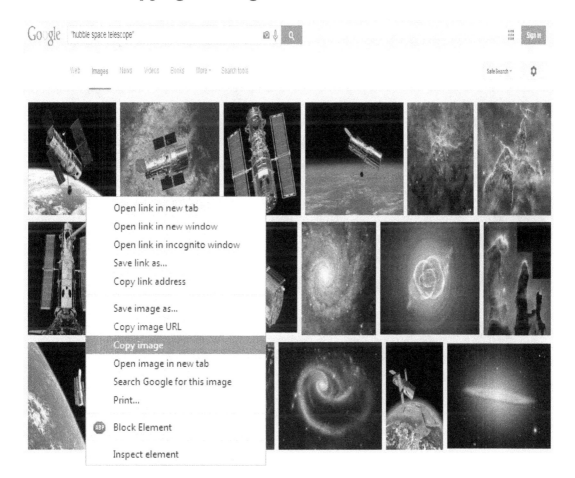

Example: **Saving an image with a right-click of the mouse.**

Search: **[hubble space telescope]**

Results: **Saving an Image – Space Station**

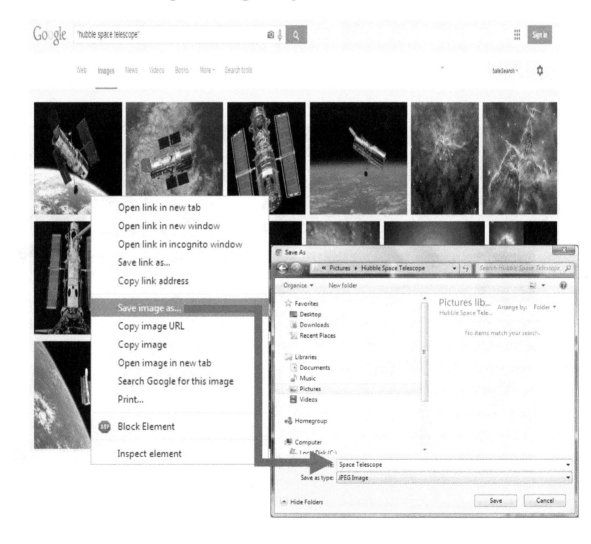

Example: **Using advanced image search features.**

Search: **[hubble space telescope]**

Results: **Search Tools – Size, Color, Type, and Usage rights**

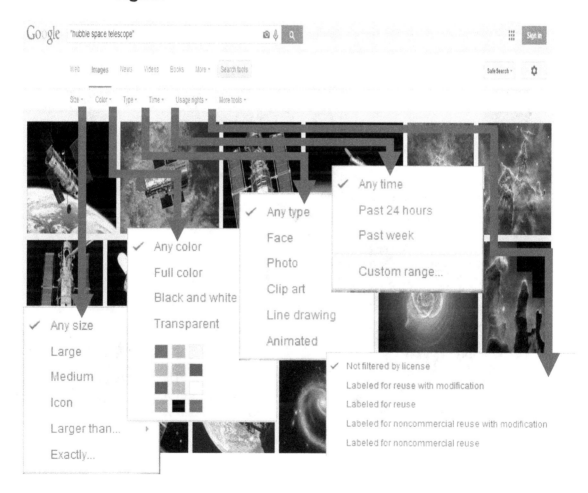

Beyond
the
Basics

Viewing
Large
Images

Example: **Viewing large-size images.**
Search: **[hubble space telescope]**
Results: **Large-size images.**

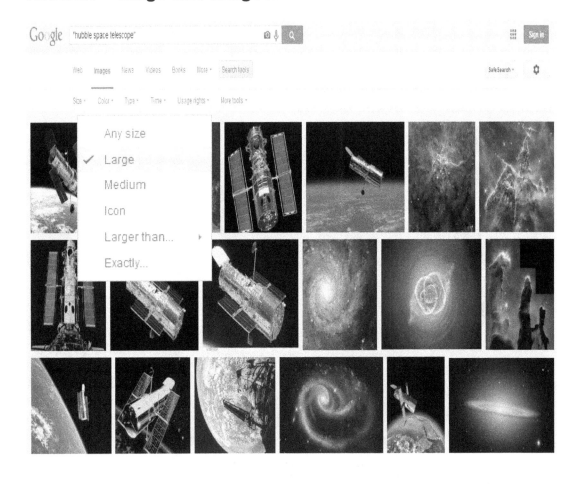

Example: **Viewing black and white images.**

Search: **[hubble space telescope]**

Results: **Images in black and white.**

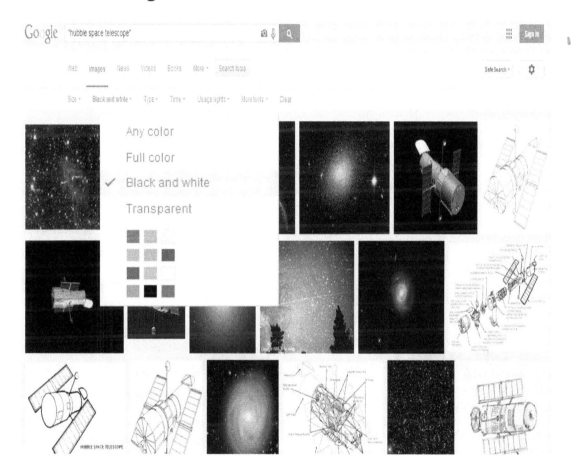

Example: **Viewing animated images.**
Search: **[hubble space telescope]**
Results: **Animated images.**

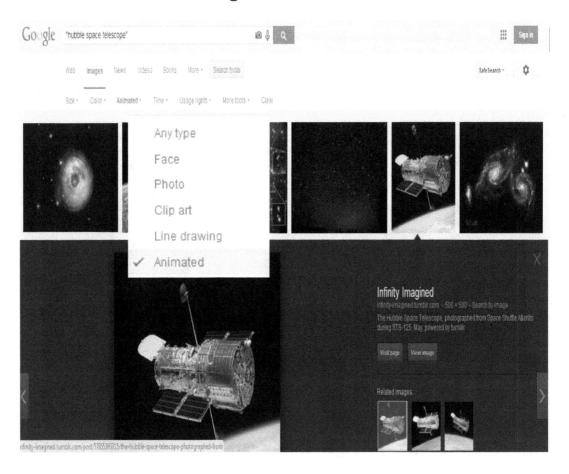

Example: **Viewing images from the past week.**

Search: **[hubble space telescope]**

Results: **Images from the past week.**

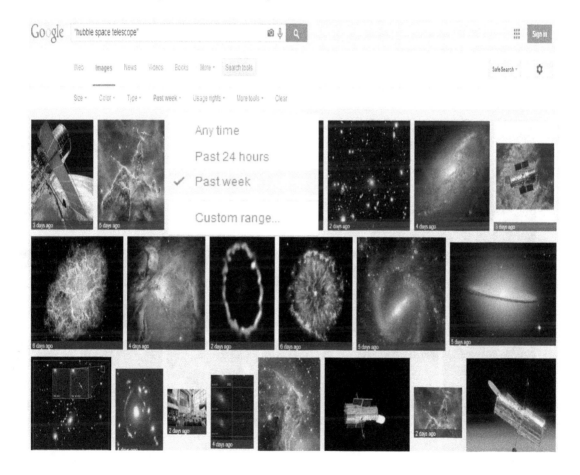

Beyond the Basics

Viewing Images for Reuse

Example: **Viewing images labeled for reuse.**
Search: **[hubble space telescope]**
Results: **Images labeled for reuse.**

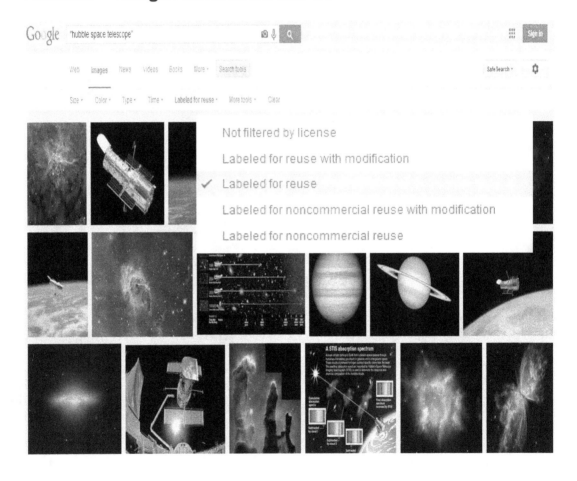

Example: **Dragging and dropping an image in the Search box.**

Search: **[hubble space telescope]**

Results: **576 results in 0.91 seconds.**

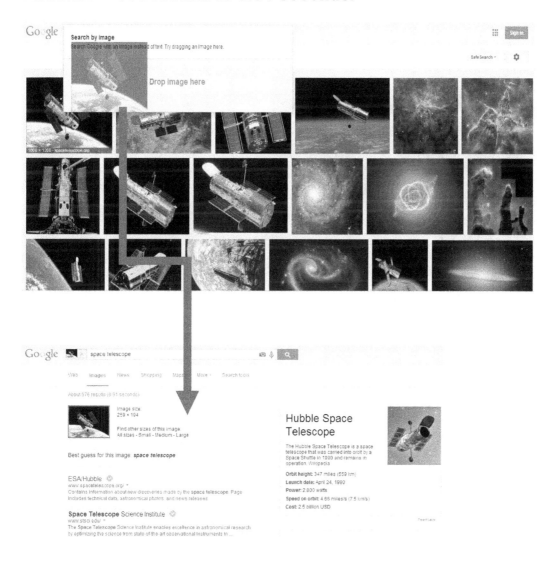

Example: **Viewing visually similar images.**

Search: **[hubble space telescope]**

Results: **Visually similar images and Pages that include Matching images.**

See results about

James Webb Space Telescope
The James Webb Space Telescope, previously known as Next Generation Space Telescope, is a ...

Visually similar images Report images

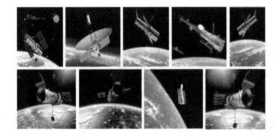

Spitzer Space Telescope
The Spitzer Space Telescope, formerly the Space Infrared Telescope Facility, is an infrared space ...

Space observatory
A space observatory is any instrument in outer space that is used for observation of distant planets, ...

Pages that include matching images

About Hubble | ESA/Hubble

www.spacetelescope.org/about/ ▾
1600 × 1200 - The Hubble Space Telescope is a collaboration between ESA and NASA. It's a long-term, space-based observatory. The observations are carried out in visible, ...

Fact Sheet | ESA/Hubble

www.spacetelescope.org › About Hubble ▾
1600 × 1200 - Fact Sheet. Hubble The Hubble Space Telescope is a joint ESA/NASA project and was launched in 1990 by the Space Shuttle mission STS-31 into a low-Earth ...

Hubble in orbit | ESA/Hubble

www.spacetelescope.org › Images ▾
1600 × 1200 - Jan 26, 2011 - This illustration shows the NASA/ESA Hubble Space Telescope in its high orbit 600 kilometres above Earth. Credit: European Space Agency ...

SearchReSearch, A Blog for Learning About Search

As fans of Google searching and image searching, one of our favorite places to go for learning about search tips, tricks, and shortcuts is a blog by Daniel M. Russell, SearchReSearch at http://searchresearch1.blogspot.com/, shown in Figure 10-2. SearchReSearch is a blog about search, search skills, teaching search, learning how to search, learning how to use Google effectively, and learning how to do research. It also covers a good deal of sensemaking and information foraging. We encourage all Google Searchers to take advantage of all the great content available on this blog.

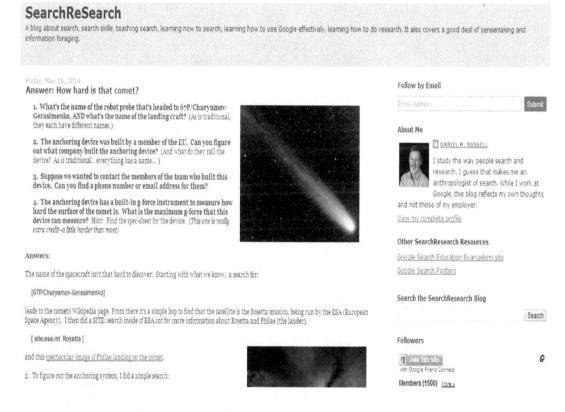

Figure 10-2. SearchReSearch Blog for Learning About Search

Section IV

References

References

An Introduction to Searching Research Databases; University of Waterloo. http://subjectguides.uwaterloo.ca/print_content.php?pid=83007&sid=616563 .

Brin, Sergey and Lawrence Page (1998). The Anatomy of a Large-Scale Hypertextual Web Search Engine. http://ilpubs.stanford.edu:8090/361/1/1998-8.pdf .

Constructing a Search Strategy; Valdosta State University; Odum Library. http://www.valdosta.edu/academics/library/tutorials/planning-your-search/constructing-a-search-strategy.php .

Farrell, Ryan (2013). A Content Marketers Guide to Google Operators (Cheat Sheet). http://www.wpromote.com/blog/seo/google-operators-infographic .

Finding Journal Articles; Illinois Institute of Technology; Paul V. Galvin Library. http://library.iit.edu/guides/databases/Databases.pdf .

Lafler, Kirk Paul and Charles Edwin Shipp (2012, 2013, 2014). Google® Search Tips and Techniques for SAS® and JMP® Users. http://www.wuss.org/proceedings12/122.pdf .

Parker, Steve Jr. (2012). Google Search Shortcuts & Tricks - Basic Tips Everyone Should Know. http://www.askingsmarterquestions.com/google-search-shortcuts-tricks-basic-tips-everyone-should-know/ .

Russell, Daniel M. (2012). How Good is Your Googling? http://searchresearch1.blogspot.com.au/2012/02/answer-where-are-you.html .

Search Strategies and Tips; University of Malawi; Chancellor College. http://www.chanco.unima.mw/library/Searching_Strategies.pdf .

References (continued)

Shapiro, David; Doug Platts and Magico Martinez (2013). Google® Hummingbird Explained. http://www.icrossing.com/sites/default/files/Google-Hummingbird-Explained-iCrossing-POV.pdf .

Section V

Keyword Index

Keyword Index

Google™ Search Complete!

Tips, Tricks and Shortcuts for Better Searches and Better Results

Kirk Paul Lafler
Charles Edwin Shipp

www.ingramcontent.com/pod-product-compliance
Lightning Source LLC
Chambersburg PA
CBHW080412060326
40689CB00019B/4220